Magnolia Mound

Front view of restored Magnolia Mound plantation home. *(Photograph by David King Gleason)*

Magnolia Mound

A LOUISIANA RIVER PLANTATION

Lois Elmer Bannon
Martha Yancey Carr
Gwen Anders Edwards

A FIREBIRD PRESS BOOK

PELICAN PUBLISHING COMPANY
Gretna 1998

To the volunteers
who have contributed
to the preservation of
Magnolia Mound Plantation

This publication has been made possible in part through a grant from the Louisiana Committee for the Humanities, a state branch of the National Endowment for the Humanities.

Library of Congress Cataloging in Publication Data

Bannon, Lois Elmer.
  Magnolia Mound.

  Bibliography: p.
  Includes index.
  1. Magnolia Mound Plantation (Baton Rouge, La.)
2. Baton Rouge (La.)—Dwellings. 3. Plantation life—
Louisiana—Baton Rouge—History. I. Carr, Martha
Yancey. II. Edwards, Gwen Anders. III. Title.
F379.B33B34   1984   976.3'18   83-7403
ISBN 0-88289-381-5

Frontispiece illustration by Stan Routh

Manufactured in the United States of America
Published by Pelican Publishing Company, Inc.
1000 Burmaster Street, Gretna, Louisiana 70053

Cover photograph by David King Gleason

Contents

List of Illustrations

Foreword

The 1960s and 1970s were eventful years in the history of Magnolia Mound plantation. The rescue and restoration of the home, as well as the early history of the site, are chronicled in this book for the first time.

What comes after the rescue and restoration of a historic site? This is what has concerned the members of the Board of Trustees of Magnolia Mound, who are responsible for policy, direction, and future planning at the plantation. With the support and cooperation of the Foundation for Historical Louisiana, the Recreation and Park Commission for the Parish of East Baton Rouge, the East Baton Rouge city-parish government, the Louisiana state government, Louisiana State University, the Junior League of Baton Rouge, and numerous other organizations and interested people in the community, much has been accomplished. It has been possible to develop an ongoing program that not only preserves but interprets the historic house and the outstanding collection of period furnishings. The outbuildings and grounds serve as a demonstration of early Louisiana plantation life from 1800 to 1830. The later structures on the site trace the evolution of the plantation and the economic system that supported it, from the original 1786 land grant to the

7

twentieth century. A sincere thank you is extended to those dedicated people who have made this a reality.

A special word of recognition and appreciation must go to the three authors who have made this work possible. Lois Elmer Bannon has served with professional expertise in directing and organizing research on Magnolia Mound since the beginning of the restoration. She is the coauthor of two books on John James Audubon: *Audubon in Louisiana* and the *Handbook of Audubon Prints*. Martha Yancey Carr, a former librarian, researched and wrote the history of the Magnolia Mound Plantation for the period from 1840 to 1960. Gwen Anders Edwards, a former university history instructor, was the director of the humanities grant that supports the publication of this chronicle.

WINIFRED EVANS BYRD
Chairman, Board of Trustees
Magnolia Mound Plantation

Acknowledgments

We gratefully thank Carol Nelson, the director of Magnolia Mound, and her staff, who gave unstintingly of their time and expertise, and the members of the Board of Trustees of Magnolia Mound, chaired by Winifred Byrd, who have strongly supported this project.

In undertaking the proper restoration of a historic house, extensive research is essential. A debt of gratitude is due to many people who contributed to the research on Magnolia Mound, which later formed the basis of this book. The response of assistance has been so overwhelming that it is impossible to name everyone.

During the tenure of Mayor W. W. (Woody) Dumas, a staunch supporter of the restoration, Ashton Stewart was the legal council for the Recreation and Park Commission for East Baton Rouge Parish (BREC) during the expropriation suit. He made available to us his significant research of conveyance records, maps, and translated Spanish colonial records. Robert Heck, architectural historian and first chairman of the board of trustees, and George Leake, the restoration architect, shared their architectural research. Sue Turner contributed research material she had collected, as well as spearheading the early progress of the major restoration as chairman of the board of

9

trustees. Evelyn Thom, who has long been involved in research on the Baton Rouge area, kept a journal when she was president of the Foundation for Historical Louisiana concerning the rescue of Magnolia Mound. The 1977 Historical Committee of the Junior League researched the early nineteenth-century kitchen under the chairmanship of Eloise Wall. Suzanne Turner, professor of landscape architecture, shared her expertise in development of the kitchen garden. Kay James, who has been on the research committee since its inception, has done much of the basic research and has also prepared an extensive chronology.

The Duplantier and Hall letters were among the most exciting discoveries. The generosity and interest of the de Combarieu family in France and Armand (A. J.) Duplantier and his son, Stephen, of New Orleans, have afforded the rare opportunity of a very personal view of plantation life in the late eighteenth and early nineteenth centuries, from the letters Armand Duplantier wrote to his family in France. Stephen Duplantier donated a fine photograph of the de Combarieu's Duplantier portrait; he and his father generously shared research for a book they are writing about Armand.

Mr. and Mrs. Charles Page of San Francisco, who first contacted us about the Hall family and have been loyal supporters of the restoration, have given copies of family letters and personal research. Elise Rosenthal, a former chairman of the board of trustees, was responsible for obtaining some of the letters donated by Hall descendants in France, Madame de Meaulne and her daughters, Francoise de Meaulne and Marie Claire Dupont. Francoise de Meaulne has also donated photographs of paintings of the plantation and portraits of the Hall family. The book *LeDoux*, written by Laverne (Pike) Thomas III, includes extensive research on the Hall family that was very useful to the project. Marilyn Domas, a dedicated member of the research committee, translated all of the Hall letters that were in French; these important documents give us a rare insight of life in the Baton Rouge area during the antebellum and Civil War periods.

Other descendants of families who owned or lived on the plantation who have given information are Jane Kelley, a Duplantier descendant, Lilac Edmiston and Pansy Levert, grandchildren of Louis Barrillier and daughters of John Aucoin, who served as overseer for Barrillier. Hardy Edmiston, Aucoin's grandson, donated the photograph of the late nineteenth-century overseer's house. Inez Searles, whose grandfather managed the plantation during part of the late nineteenth century, and her son R. Jesse Searles provided information on the later years of the plantation. Anna Belle Anderson has generously contributed, among other things, the copy of the important 1880 map of the plantation. Fannie Reynaud, Marion LeBlanc, and Mrs. Anderson, all descendants of Robert Hart, have helped us in researching the Hart family years. Mrs. LeBlanc has also assisted with research of all of the conveyance records.

The archaeological excavations by Dr. William Haag of Louisiana State University and his students and by Coastal Environments, Inc., have revealed valuable information. Dr. and Mrs. Jack Holden have assisted in locating sources for decorative art and lifestyle research. H. Parrot Bacot, curator of the Anglo-American Museum at Louisiana State, has served as consultant to Magnolia Mound in the acquisition of its significant collection of furniture and accessories. He has given freely of his time, expertise, and scholarship. George Castille, Ernest Gueymard, Daniel Turnbull, Powell Casey, and the late St. Clair Favrot have shared information from their own research. Cynthia Cash gathered material essential for our description of the antebellum plantation layout and lifestyle. (This study was done for the "Master Site Development Plan," executed in 1981 by Jon Emerson of Unicorn Studio.) The late Leland Richardson assisted with legal research. Wing Sigler, former curator of Magnolia Mound, Lucile Munson, Lucile O'Brien, and Florence Gregorie translated French and Spanish documents; Nathalie diBenedetto deciphered virtually illegible handwritten documents. Throughout the years of research, Mary Harvey typed hundreds of copies of documents, many originals of which were almost illegible. Alain LeVasseur accomplished important research in France and also contributed photographs.

Wanda Barber, Winifred Byrd, Lillie Coleman, Ann West, and the 1976 Junior League Historical Committee, chaired by Charlene Kennedy, have worked with the research committee. Dr. William Cooper has given us his expert guidance as has M. Stone Miller, Jr., and Mary Jane Kahao. Karen Corkern, Dr. Daniel Littlefield, Rosalind McKenzie, and Joan Samuel have also been of assistance. Pat Smylie helped edit the final draft of the manuscript.

Institutions whose staffs have given generously of their time and service are the Troy H. Middleton Library at Louisiana State University, particularly the archives department and the Louisiana Room; the East Baton Rouge Parish Main Library and Centroplex branch; the Louisiana Department of the Louisiana State Library; the Mobile, Alabama, Public Library; the Mobile County Courthouse and Archives; the East Baton Rouge Parish Courthouse; and the Pointe Coupee Parish Courthouse.

Introduction

It was 1967. Magnolia Mound was saved! The torrential rain poured from the black Louisiana sky as the first board members met at the old plantation house. As rain dripped over their umbrellas, they stood huddled together in the bare parlor, silently watching the water trickle over the hand-carved moldings and ceiling rosette. The vote was unanimous—the first money they could raise would be for a new roof. The battle was over, and the slow process of restoration began.

Researching the social and architectural history of the plantation was the first step in planning the restoration. This book is about that history and the history of the house and grounds from the beginning of the restoration to the present. Planned to satisfy the visitor who desires more information than a handout brochure provides, this book forms a stepping stone for scholarly research. The historiography is enhanced by accounts of some of the social, political, and scientific events that affected the evolution of Magnolia Mound plantation as it developed from a settler's house and farm first to a large house within an extensive working plantation, then to a suburban residence, and finally to a public historic site.

LOIS ELMER BANNON

13

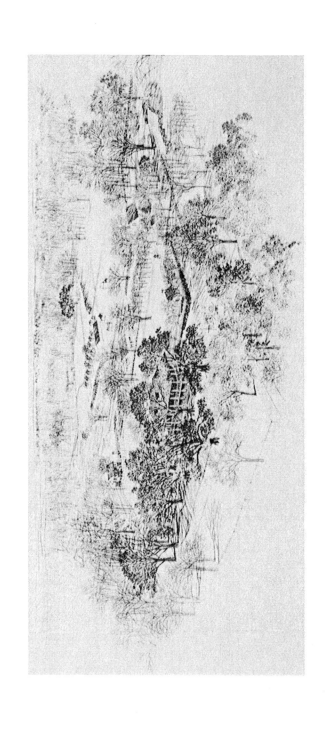

PART I

CHAPTER I
@꧁◉꧂@
Prelude

The high ridge along the Mississippi River in the Baton Rouge area was formed during the last ice age of the Pleistocene period from the outwash of the glacier that carved out the river and huge river valley. Magnolia Mound, like many local houses, is situated on this ridge. It is one of the survivors of the late eighteenth century, and through a study of the old structure, as a three-dimensional historic relic, we can learn much about history. We have an opportunity to be involved in a kind of time travel. We can walk through a house built for a special climate and the particular river plantation way of life. The home is situated near old Baton Rouge, a little fort that grew to be part of one of the world's largest petrochemical areas, in reasonable traveling distance from New Orleans, the river's gateway to the world.

Magnolia Mound's history is the history of the area. Extensive research has revealed evidence of prehistoric and historic Indians, explorers, colonizers and settlers, plantation owners, slaves, and employees, and shown the involvement of investors, urban developers, preservationists, and educators. Architectural investigation, archaeological excavations, and historical documents piece together a fascinating story of a river plantation—a story not complete, and in some instances perhaps not correct. Present and future generations will make further contributions to this continuing story.

The first evidence of man on the Magnolia Mound property comes from shards found in recent archaeological excavations. They are dated from the Cole's Creek period (A.D. 700–1100), and represent a culture that extended beyond the northern boundaries of the state of Louisiana.

During the 1850s, when George Hall resided at Magnolia Mound, a crude archaeological dig took place in an "Indian mound" on the property. In a letter to the Baton Rouge *Comet,* Hall's son wrote:

> As a great deal of curiosity has existed with regard to the contents of the Magnolia Mound, a beautiful relic of the aborigines, situated to the left of Highland Road, near the residence of Mr. George O. Hall, a party of gentlemen proceeded to the spot on Sunday last, with a body of eight stout negroes armed with picks and spades and a canteen of the needful; and at the base of the mound under the cool shade of the beautiful magnolias, proceeded to dig into it.
>
> The difficulty encountered at the outset from the luxuriant vegetation was soon removed, and we then proceeded with tepid strides into the body of the mound. After an hour's work we met with the obstruction of a stone wall, composed of large round, water-washed pebbles, cemented together into a symmetrical mass of perfect workmanship: We proceeded to dig about it and found it to be of a triangular form having upon its surface a large slab of limestone, nearly spherical, which on removing the earth we found to contain curious hieroglyphics, divided into four segments. To what use could such a block be put by the savages who inhabited this section of the country at its discovery? This question naturally occurred to us, but where was the solution?
>
> After much labor, we succeeded in removing the slab from the masonry, which we found to be closed at the top in such a manner as to defy the pickaxe. We reluctantly gave up the work, but to be resumed again in a few days. In

the meantime such of your citizens as desire to examine
the work can do so prior to its removal to New Orleans.

This archaeological excavation will surely make
present-day archaeologists shudder. We will never know
what valuable information was shoveled away; nor is there
a clue about where the limestone slab was taken in New
Orleans. Dr. W. G. Haag, an archaeologist from Louisiana
State University who has supervised several of the recent
Magnolia Mound excavations, thinks that this mound was
probably from the Poverty Point culture, which was earlier
than Cole's Creek.

The historic Indians who later had villages near the
Baton Rouge area were the Houma, the Tunica, and the
Bayougoula. All of these tribes were known to the French
explorers, who bestowed the name "Red Stick" on the

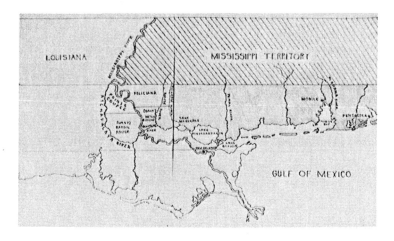

Figure 1. Spanish West Florida, the Gulf coast region below thirty-
one degrees longitude, stretched from the Florida of today
west to the Mississippi River. Ruled by the Spanish until
1763, the area including Baton Rouge came under British
control, although it was soon returned to Spanish domination. *(Drawing by Karen Corkern)*

Houma's village perched on a bluff on the Mississippi River several miles north of what was to become Magnolia Mound plantation.

The French and Spanish explorers traversed the river in this vicinity, and the French claimed the area along with the rest of the huge Louisiana territory in 1682. Their attempt to colonize the Baton Rouge area was a dismal failure. That portion of Louisiana was acquired by the British in 1763, as a result of the Treaty of Paris at the conclusion of the Seven Years' War. Spain also ceded East and West Florida to Great Britain, so that a large area of the east side of the river became anglicized (figure 1). Baton Rouge, called Fort Richmond by the British, prospered under their rule. However, there are no records of British activity on the Magnolia Mound site. Many British colonials who were loyal to their king moved into the area to avoid involvement in the American Revolution, but they did not remain British citizens long. In 1779 Spain and Great Britain were again at war, and Bernardo de Galvez won Baton Rouge from the British.

CHAPTER II

⚜️◉⚜️

The Beginning
Of A River Plantation

The first recorded information about the Magnolia Mound property appears in the Spanish colonial records of the late eighteenth century, when Spain was actively encouraging the settling of its colonies. On December 12, 1786, James Hillin acquired a land grant for the property. An idea of what he did with it in the next four years can be gleaned from the records of the succession at his wife's death. From Jane Stanley Hillin's succession one can visualize a settler's house, dependencies, and grounds. There must have been quarters for slaves, but they are not recorded; the slaves themselves were much more valuable than their cabins. This early document gives the name of each slave's African nation of origin, an important consideration in determining his value. (The house described in the succession inventory is not the house existing today. The description that fits the first phase of the restored Magnolia Mound will appear in a later document.)

The inventory gives the impression of a farm with cows, pigs, working animals, a few slaves, and a tobacco crop. In discussing agriculture in lower Louisiana ten years after Hillin acquired his land grant, James Pitot wrote in

Observation on the Colony of Louisiana:

> Spain should have undertaken long ago to improve agri-
> culture in the province of Louisiana, and to prepare in
> advance for the competition that all European govern-
> ments ought to give to the United States for possession of
> Louisiana. . . . Plug tobacco: Its production had been
> encouraged by a contract to fill the needs of the mother
> country, but the king or his agents suspended their pur-
> chases. In recent years the tobacco planter offered it for
> quite a while to merchants, but they could not handle it
> profitably. He finally sold it at distress prices to cover his
> expenses, and retired to the bosom of his family where he
> could hide his misery and chagrin.

Apparently Hillin had planted tobacco when it was still
economically sound to do so. Indigo, too, had become a
money crop by this time, and Hillin cultivated it, as did
Magnolia Mound's next owner, John Joyce.

In 1791 Hillin sold the property to Joyce, a resident of
Mobile, which was also a Spanish possession. In the act of
sale Joyce claimed to be a resident of Baton Rouge,
perhaps because he and a business partner had previously
purchased property in the Baton Rouge area. Armand
Duplantier, who would later reside at Magnolia Mound,
was a witness to the sale.

John Joyce emigrated to Mobile from County Cork,
Ireland. His wife, Constance Rochon, was a Creole, a first-
generation native of the colonies, whose parents had emigrated from France. In Mobile Joyce was in the mercantile business with John Turnbull, the father of Rosedown
plantation's Daniel Turnbull. Joyce and Turnbull can best
be described as eighteenth-century wheeler-dealers. They
had a suburban branch of their mercantile establishment
for the Indians who resided outside of the village, and
Turnbull had an Indian family there. Together and
individually they owned property throughout the North
American Spanish colonies. Joyce was also in the
construction business. Specific buildings that he com-

pleted in 1793 are noted in the Mobile colonial records: a church, a parsonage, and a large wharf.

Magnolia Mound became an absentee-owned property probably supervised by an overseer, an indispensable employee on a plantation. Joyce must have traveled to Baton Rouge from Mobile by a popular route from the Gulf of Mexico through the lakes and Bayou Manchac to the Mississippi River, and then a short trip upriver or over-land to Magnolia Mound. It is likely that he sometimes returned via New Orleans, because he could travel down-river all the way. Joyce had property in New Orleans, and there was always business to attend to in the port city, which was the seat of the governor of the province. No records have been located to suggest how often Joyce

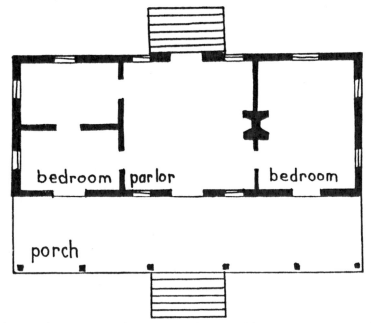

Figure 2. This floor plan shows architectural historians' conjectured re-creation of the original Magnolia Mound house, com-pleted during John Joyce's ownership (1791–1798).

visited his Baton Rouge property or whether or not his family ever accompanied him.

The house located on the property today was built during Joyce's ownership. It does not appear on the Hillin act of sale; but Hillin's house and another house that fits the description of the first stage of the house that stands today appear in Joyce's succession. As Joyce was a contractor, he might have built the second structure, a four-room house typical of the Franco-Spanish style in the Louisiana settlement during the late eighteenth and early nineteenth centuries—no hallways, large doors and windows arranged to provide cross-ventilation in the hot summer, a back-to-back chimney to provide warmth in the mild winters, and a front porch (figure 2). All of the original walls that still exist are constructed of stakes and *bousillage,* an excellent insulator composed of mud and moss (figure 3). The highly pitched cypress-shingled roof with ample eaves and the cypress pillars that raised the house well off the ground gave protection from the humid, rainy weather of southern Louisiana.

When Joyce purchased the plantation in 1791, indigo was still a major money crop. The indigo cultivated in Louisiana was the same type as that grown in the West Indies; these two New World regions competed with India for the world indigo market. The blue green leaf of this tall plant resembles an acacia leaf and produces a dark blue dye after it has been processed.

The production process began when slaves cut the leaves from the plant with sickles before the stem became woody. They carried bundles of leaves to the indigo shed, where an experienced operator was in charge. The leaves were placed in a vat, covered with water, and left to steep for several hours until a froth appeared on them. The water and residue formed from the rotting leaves was let through a bunghole in the lower vat, where the contents were agitated by slaves using some type of mixing and

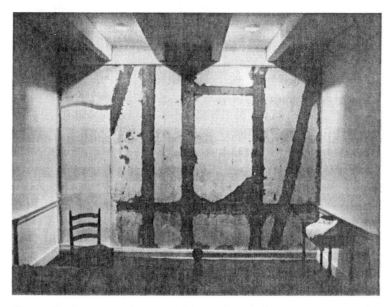

Figure 3. An exposed section of *bousillage* wall construction is visible in the children's bedroom of the restored Magnolia Mound house. *(Photograph by David King Gleason)*

plunging device, usually large iron or wooden forks. The agitating took place in the battery vat, where the famous indigo silver cup was used: "The water, when it is all in the second vat, is beat till the indigo-operator gives orders to cease; which he does not before he has several times taken up some of this water with a silver cup, by way of assay, in order to know the exact time in which they ought to give over beating the water; and this is a secret which practice alone can teach with certainty." The operator knew when to stop agitation by the color of the liquid in the silver cup.

When the beating had ceased, the liquid was allowed to settle. A thick substance remained on the bottom and the water was drained off. The substance was then let into the last and lowest vat. From there it was placed in cloth bags and hung on nails around the indigo shed, so that the remaining water could drip out. When the substance was removed from the cloth, it was spread into rectangular molds about twenty-four inches by six inches. The molds were placed in the sun to dry, and while the "cakes" were fresh, they were cut into cubes called "junks."

In 1798 a plantation owner across the river in Pointe Coupee wrote to his brother in France complaining about the pitiful indigo harvest. He was Armand Duplantier, who would later become master of Magnolia Mound. The story was the same all through the colonies: indigo was out and cotton was in. John Joyce, who was a much more astute businessman than Duplantier, had already converted Magnolia Mound to a primarily cotton plantation. Not only was indigo having unfavorable seasons, but it was producing rust in wheat, it had considerable competition in the world market, and its manufacture seemed to injure the health of the slaves (indigo is now thought to be a carcinogen). Cotton was easier to plant and care for than indigo—so much so that even young slaves were able to help harvest. The slaves preferred to work a cotton plantation above all others. James Pitot wrote in the 1790s:

> Cotton was then replanted in the colony, and the first efforts in that new cultivation were guided rather by necessity than hope of success, since tradition regarding earlier attempts could serve to discourage it. Nevertheless, agreeably surprised with the results, their labor, far from being lost as it had been for many years in the crops of indigo, was rewarded. Immediately followed by those who through fear, preoccupation, or discouragement of misfortune had kept in idleness, they saw an annual increase in the products of a soil that was thought worn-out, and gins and presses were established and improved for the exploitation of that commodity. They harvested about one thousand pounds of seed cotton per arpent [.85 acre], and cultivated at least three arpents with each laborer. Ease then finally took the place of want among a great many planters, and wealth soon banished financial embarrassment and privations among several others. Circum-

stances made the price of cotton increase and stay at the highest level; and in a country where a few years earlier agriculture did not provide enough for commerce to half fill the small number of ships that brought in the colony's supplies, one saw a growing number coming in ballast to take on cargo.

On February 24, 1798, Joyce and Turnbull filed a partnership agreement in New Orleans, legalizing their partnership of many years and adding much of their individual properties to it. Turnbull had left Mobile by this time and taken up residence in the district of Baton Rouge. It looked as though 1798 was going to be another good year for Joyce and Turnbull, but it turned out to be their last. The story of Joyce's death is found in the translated West Florida records, when Nicholas Cook was interrogated through an interpreter by the commandant of Fort Mobile on May 10, 1798.

Asking him his name, where he was a native from and what was his occupation, he answered that his name was Nicholas Cook, that he is a native of Scotland and that at present he has the command of a schooner of his belonging named *The Mobilian*. That he comes from a trip from the city of New Orleans.

Being asked to give a detailed information of all the happenings concerning the unfortunate death of John Joyce, the interpreter said that he so asked him, and the witness answered: that on the night of the 9th, about eleven o'clock, he anchored in front of Round Island, with a heavy sea, the waves were very high. That the deceased Joyce, on account of the excessive heat inside, insisted on sleeping where it would be cool upon the round-house, of which intention the declarant could not persuade him not to follow, that the deceased ordered a negro to bring up his mattress, and he lay down. The declarant having had a sleepless night the previous night, did exactly the same, but towards the bow of the schooner, and in this stage of affairs, about 2 A.M., the chaplain, Juan de Dios Valdes, who was a passenger in the schooner, woke him up, calling him to get up, because he could hear a voice at sea, that was

John Joyce's voice. That the declarent getting up they
went to the place where Joyce had been sleeping, who
they did not find anywhere in the schooner. That they
heard at a distance the voice of a man who was drowning.

On being interrogated about the efforts they made to
help the said Joyce, he said that immediately he prepared
the pirogue to launch it, but that the night being too dark,
the sea so rough, and the waves too violent, and not
hearing the voices anymore, he considered that it would be
useless to look for him, due to the fact that the waves were
taking away and by that time he was probably drowned.

Being equally interrogated who were the passengers,
and the crew, he answered through the interpreter that the
passengers were, Chaplain Juan de Dios Valdes, Isam
Beard, and a negro slave of the said John Joyce. The other
passengers gave a similar account.

In September of that same year, Turnbull died at his
residence in what records term "the district of Baton
Rouge." The widows of the two business partners were left
to separate the property with the aid of Charles Norwood,
the executor. Curators were appointed for their children's
interests: Jacques Guinault was appointed curator of
Josephine and William Joyce and Armand Duplantier, the
captain of the militia, was named curator of the Turnbull
children. Constance Joyce came to Baton Rouge to
participate in the inventories of the properties. Among the
properties that she inherited was the plantation near
Baton Rouge later known as Magnolia Mound. She also
inherited other properties and about one hundred slaves.
Madame Joyce was a wealthy widow.

CHAPTER III

⊛⊰◎⊱⊛

The Plantation Gentry:
The Duplantier Years

The widow of John Joyce resided in Mobile but often visited her Baton Rouge properties. In 1802 she married Armand Duplantier, himself a widower with four children, and they settled on Constance's Baton Rouge plantation. They remodeled and enlarged the house to accommodate their new family, which consisted of Constance Joyce and her two children, Josephine and William, and Armand and his three-year-old daughter, Augustine, and his oldest son, Fergus. His other two sons, Armand and Guy, were in France (figure 4).

Constance and Armand modernized their home in the "federal" style popular at that time. The elaborate handmade cove ceiling with the wood rosette in the parlor, the hand-carved moldings in the principal rooms, and the federal-style mantels were installed at that time. The house was extended to the rear to include a dining room, rooms on both sides, and a back gallery. Two rooms were added on the south side, and the front gallery was extended (figure 5). The exterior walls were overlaid with plaster. The parlor and probably the dining room were wallpapered. Some original hardware, including scroll hinges and drop latches, still exist from this period. In the attic the construction of both the eighteenth and early

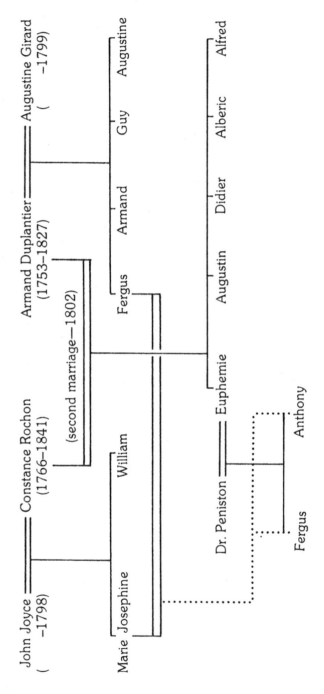

(Key: double lines indicate marriage; single lines offspring; dotted lines adoption.)

Figure 4. Family tree showing the descendants of the Joyce and Duplantier families of Magnolia Mound.

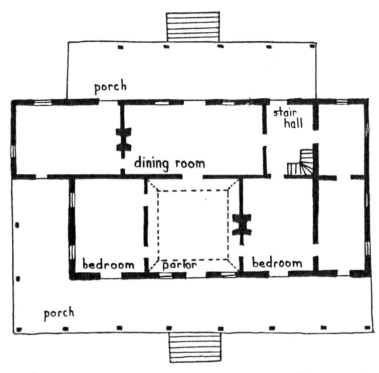

Figure 5. The Duplantier family made extensive additions to the original Magnolia Mound house in the early 1800s to provide for their children, as this floor plan shows.

nineteenth centuries can be seen. The Spanish colonial records of 1804 refer to this Duplantier plantation as Magnolia Mound.

The new master of Magnolia Mound, Armand Duplantier, was a prominent colonial citizen (figure 6). He was born in 1753 in Voiron, France, and came to America to serve with Lafayette during the American Revolution. He came to Louisiana in 1781 to assist his maternal uncle, Claude Trenonay, with his plantation in Pointe Coupee, an area across the river from Baton Rouge. It is fortunate that the de Combarieus of France, collateral descendants of Armand Duplantier, have in their possession letters

Figure 6. Inscribed "Armand Duplantier, En Amerique," the original of this painting is owned by Duplantier descendants in France. According to family tradition, the portrait was sent to France between 1783 and 1785. However, historical experts on clothing and textiles place the style around 1805 to 1810; the subject could therefore be Armand Duplantier, Jr.

from Trenonay and Duplantier to their relatives in France. From these letters one can read the hopes and frustrations of a young man colonizing on a frontier far from his family and native country. Armand's uncle had married a widow; Armand's first wife was her daughter, Augustine Gerard. The uncle and nephew did not get along as well as they had hoped, and the younger couple, with the aid of Augustine's inheritance, purchased their own plantation. Armand's initial plans were to make enough money for his family to return to France.

Trenonay was murdered in 1792 by a slave, and Armand spent several frustrating years administering his uncle's succession. The colonists were victims of the international power politics of France, England, and Spain, and it was difficult to communicate with the heirs in France and obtain documents necessary for the estate settlement. In the colony itself it was almost impossible for Armand to keep up with the legal red tape because of ever-changing officials and governments.

The French Revolution discouraged Armand from returning to France, although he was concerned about his sons' lack of education. Augustine did her best to tutor them, but in 1799 she died of yellow fever, leaving Armand to rear three sons and a five-week-old daughter, little Augustine. Even before his wife's death he had complained in a letter to his sister that he hoped it was not too late to provide his little daughter with a dowry, that his sons have "no education and no talent for anything but planting," that he was having difficulty with the slaves, and that the crops had been poor. His share of his uncle's estate was also a great disappointment. When the planned retrocession of the colony to France became known in 1802, Armand again made plans to return to France. In June, 1802, he sent to France two of his sons, seventeen-year-old Armand and twelve-year-old Guy, to be educated there under the care of his brother.

In the fall of 1802 he wrote to his sister that he had married Madame Joyce, a wealthy widow of whom he had spoken for several years, and that she was a good person who would make a fine mother for Augustine. He also wrote that his Creole wife would find life in France very different from the colony, and that she could profit from lessons in housekeeping from his sister.

In the village of Baton Rouge, Jacques Guinault, the curator of the Joyce children, was causing quite a brouhaha about Constance Joyce's marriage and the disposition of her crops. The translator of the Spanish West Florida records summed up the numerous documents:

> The longest litigation involving the largest [dual] estate that has appeared in the West Florida records, apparently is the partition sale of the widows of John Turnbull and John Joyce. The original documents of the above mentioned sale are in Volume III. . . . The partition sale of the widows Turnbull and Joyce involves the names of most of the prominent men in governmental, financial, and ecclesiastical circles in New Orleans, Mobile, and Baton Rouge. . . .
>
> Jacques Philippe Guinault, curator ad litem of the Joyce minors, was the author of many letters seemingly for the sole purpose of ascertaining the truth of the mother's rumored marriage. So persistent was Guinault that Governor Salcedo issued an order to Governor Grand Pre to ascertain the facts. An Irish priest educated for the priesthood in Spain, and sent with others of his native country to attend to the spiritual wants of the English speaking settlers of West Florida, was said to have performed the ceremony. In reply to Grand Pre's letter of inquiry, Padre Lennon, formerly priest of the church at Baton Rouge, later located at the church of the Second Coast of the German [St. John the Baptist] replied that he had officiated at the marriage of Constance Rochon Joyce and Armand Allard Duplantier, but fails to mention the date of the ceremony.

During Armand Duplantier's years as master of Magnolia Mound, the Duplantiers' financial affairs deteriorated because of the tumultuous international situation, mismanagement, and bad investments. From 1807 until 1814 Armand owned part of the DeLord-Sarpy plantation, including the beautiful house and furnishings, in Faubourg Hagen, a nineteenth-century New Orleans suburb. Legal documents and a letter written by Duplantier to his brother show that he lost this investment because of his unfortunate financial situation. On January 24, 1803, he wrote that a ship carrying Duplantier cotton, apparently bound for France, had been stopped at sea. He feared that the cotton would be sold in England, where his profits might be lost. In the same letter he wrote, "The Americans intend to take over tomorrow and people are waiting to see the outcome." He wrote that he had sold his plantation and slaves but still had his wife's property. A month later he wrote that they were still awaiting the arrival of the French. He noted that the price of Negroes had fallen, that sending mail, especially money, was difficult because of the war, and that "the Spanish government is issuing no money."

A January, 1804, letter written in New Orleans to his brother states, "The Americans have had possession of the colony for more than a month. Colonists are impatiently awaiting the installation of the new government, which will give them neutrality and port advantages." In a history of Baton Rouge, J. St. Clair Favrot tells of this period.

> The event which brought the most unrest to this section of Louisiana was the transfer of Louisiana from Spain to France by the Treaty of San Ildefonso in 1801 and its subsequent sale by France to the United States in 1803. Loud were the cries of the pro-American partisans living in the area between Bayou Manchac and the Mississippi line on learning they were not to become citizens of the United States but were to remain part of Spanish West Florida. Only the pro-Spanish, a small minority, were pleased, while pro-French and pro-British adherents joined with the unhappy Americans. . . .

As far back as 1804, there had been rumblings against the Spaniards and in August of that year, a group of Americans under the leadership of Reuben Kemper published a declaration of independence . . . and set out to capture Governor Don Carlos de Grand Pre at Baton Rouge.

That capture was thwarted by a group of soldiers led by none other than Armand Duplantier, captain of the militia. When West Florida finally did become part of the United States, Duplantier made an exemplary citizen, and served in the War of 1812. His obituary in the October 1827 Baton Rouge *Gazette* indicates that his peers held him in high esteem.

[Died] at his seat, near this place, on Sunday 30th of September at 8 o'clock A.M.—Joseph Armand Allard Duplantier Sen. Esq., aged 74. The deceased was a native of Voiron, Dept. of Isere, in France; and was in the service of his native country as an officer of cavalry at the commencement of our Revolutionary War, when obeying the finest impulses of the human heart that actuated so many of his countrymen, he joined the French army sent to our relief; and served as Captain several years in our Continental army under command of the great and good Lafayette of whom he was the intimate friend in arms, and whose highest esteem he ever deserved and enjoyed. Yielding to the solicitations of an uncle who resided in Louisiana he came to this territory in 1781, where he has since resided. By his active industry he acquired considerable property, which, however, was soon wrested from him by unforseen and uncontrollable reverses of fortune. At an advanced age this patriarch was enjoying the enviable satisfaction of seeing all of his children happily settled in life, when the premature death 18 months since of a fondly cherished daughter broke in upon the serenity of his calm and unruffled life. This dispensation of Providence, notwithstanding his fortitude, and resignation of which he possessed a large share, was too afflicting for one who loved so tenderly and who was so far advanced in years.

Few men possessed in a higher degree the qualities essential in a character to command our esteem in private life; he was a warm and sincere friend never treating the

feelings of characters of his fellow citizens lightly;
charitable to the poor, and a bright example in the different
characters of husband, father and master.

It may with truth be said he never had but friends, as he
always treated those of whom he might justly complain, as
if he made the Golden Rule the test of all his actions.

A gratifying and honest proof of the estimation in which
Mr. Duplantier was held by those who knew him best, was
furnished by the large and respectable concourse of his
fellow citizens who attended his remains to the place of
interment, and notwithstanding the length of the road, the
dust and heat were excessive, the United States Troops
stationed at the post moved as an escort in procession in
order to pay him military honors, and to render a last
tribute of gratitude to one of the fathers of our
independence.

Armand and Constance Duplantier had never moved to
France. They had remained at Magnolia Mound, where
she had borne him five children, a daughter, Euphemie,
and four sons, Augustin, Didier, Alberic, and Alfred.

Fergus Duplantier did visit France for a few years. After
he returned to Louisiana, he married his stepsister,
Josephine Joyce, and through her inheritance he acquired
the south portion of Magnolia Mound plantation. Fergus
and Josephine had no children, but they later adopted
their deceased half-sister's children, Fergus and Anthony
Peniston. Fergus Peniston (Duplantier by adoption) is best
known for having built Chatsworth plantation house.

What were the manners and customs of the people who
resided in the Louisiana river plantations during the
Duplantier years? "Louisiana Revisited," researched by
Martha Carr and written by Gwen Edwards for the
Magnolia Mound docents, gives us an interesting answer:

"In the late eighteenth and nineteenth centuries a
popular literary form was travelers' accounts of their
impressions of visits to unfamiliar areas. Used with care,
these accounts, along with journals, can be valuable
sources for knowledge of lifestyles and customs seen by

contemporary eyes. Four such sources are used to take a glimpse backward into the time frame of the early development of Magnolia Mound.

"John Pintard, a cultured New York merchant, left an account of his visit to New Orleans in 1801. He found the city unimpressive at first sight and deplored the filth of streets and canals. But after sampling the hospitality and visiting more of the city, he found much to admire. He recognized the growing importance and vitality of the city, influenced by its location as the gateway to the vast river system that bisected the continent. The people living along it referred to it merely as 'the River,' unconsciously denoting that it ran through their lives as well as their lands. The deep, rich alluvial soil deposited along its banks was partially responsible for the fabled wealth eventually produced by the plantation economy.

"This factor was duly noted in the journal of a traveler from South Carolina, who left a day-by-day account of his trip up the Mississippi to New Orleans and on eventually to Natchez. 'It is impossible to conceive any soil richer than it is on Each side. . . . Nothing is put in the ground that don't grow in the most luxuriant manner,' he wrote.

"All of these accounts describe the river traffic and the number of barges, bateaus, and boats of all descriptions plying the waters upriver from New Orleans—an area commonly designated as 'the Coast.' Individual travel, however, by planters between New Orleans and as far upriver as Baton Rouge, was often on horseback or by some land vehicle, not always by water. And any hapless traveler caught by nightfall, whether friend or stranger, was assured of hospitality from the nearest family, given lodging and a bounteous meal and sped on his way by morning," the Edwards article continues.

"The South Carolina traveler, Dr. John Sibley, continued his journey upriver, leaving a graphic description, albeit in poor grammar and even poorer spelling, of his experiences and observations. His was an uncertain journey begun on a barge. If he were not aboard when time came to push off the next morning, he was left on his own resources. So sometimes he walked, occasionally he was lent a horse, and once he pushed his baggage in a cart until he overtook the barge again. But invariably he was graciously received when he knocked on the nearest planter's house, and he left a description of life and manners of this era.

> The Barge landed on the W. Side of the River after Sundown Six leagues from Town . . . and I got a mulatto Boy who spoke French and English to go with me to a French gentleman's house near where we Landed where I asked to Stay the Night. . . .
>
> An Old Gentleman met me at the Steps, shook me by Hand and Gave me a hearty welcome and envited me to Sit down in the Gallery. . . . The Old Gentleman spoke no English, his name was DePann [translator states that this was probably Destrehan], appeared to be very Rich from the number of Servants, furniture, Plate and buildings he had—soon after I sat down I had lay'd my hat on a Table the Old Man brought my hat and put it on my head and told me in French that the dew was unwholesome and then retired into his Room. . . .
>
> The Old Gentleman did not appear again till Supper was announc'd in the Great Hall. The Table was elegantly set, and a variety of Dishes of Meat, Sassages, Hashes, Stews, Sallads, Vegetables and with Handsome plate, Silver forks, Spoons, etc. a Variety of Wines, but none but Claret was touched. . . .
>
> During Supper and for an hour after he Conversed freely on Medicine and the Small Pox which had been thro his family, it getting late withdrew as I afterwards discovred to Examine if my Room was ready, and a servant was directed to show me the Room which I found in the neatest Order, a Clean Handkerchief for my head, wine and water. On the Toilet a Guglet Bason and Towell on a stand with Powder Combs, Pomatum, etc., and some Books.
>
> As I intended to start by day light for fear the Barge would not wait for me I went immediately to the bed soon

after the Old Man came to my door and asked me, couchee
Monsieur (are you in Bed, Sir)? I answered him in the affir-
mative, he then told me Bon Repose. I saw no more of him.

Thus, he wrote, was he received every night on his way up
'the River' for ten or twelve nights.

"Several days later he stopped at Philip Hickey's plantation just below Baton Rouge and noted that Hickey was an
Irishman 'remarkable for his good living and Hospitality, is
very rich and keeps up a great degree of Sociableness in
the neighborhood.' He was impressed with the variety of
wine and liquors on the sideboard and commented that
'the Old Gentleman kept the wine moving got very merry,
sat up late and insisted on putting me to bed himself.' *Bon
Repose,* indeed. Philip Hickey was a prominent planter in
the Baton Rouge area and the owner of Hope Estate just
downriver from Magnolia Mound.

"The next day Sibley cryptically records, 'The Barge had
to stop to deliver some goods at Mr. Rowels a Mile above
and at Madam Joyce's.' This has to be Magnolia Mound's
Constance Rochon Joyce, for the time and location fit.
(This entry in the journal was penned in early October,
1802, and she and Armand Duplantier were married by
late October, 1802.) Would that Dr. Sibley had arrived at
Magnolia Mound at dusk and knocked on the door and
asked for lodging and left a description of his hospitable
reception, mentioning the plate and liquors on the sideboard. At the very least he could have recorded what kind
of goods were delivered. But such are the disappoint-
ments and near misses of historical research.

"The river was a part of the planters' environment as
well as an important resource; but although it could be
beneficial, it could also be an implacable foe. Though the
spring floods left a deposit of rich alluvial soil, the more
tangible result was the havoc wreaked on lands, property,
and pocketbooks. Also the lower reaches of the
Mississippi formed into bayous, swamps, marshes, and

shallow lakes that make breeding grounds for mos-
quitoes, insects, and fever-producing 'miasmas.' So
Louisiana, more than most frontier areas, had its health
problems, and there were regular outbreaks of malaria,
typhus, dysentery, and yellow fever. Family letters and
early newspapers are filled with accounts of sickness, and
death was an ever-present specter. The travelers'
accounts take due note of this; in fact they remark on the
healthiness of the inhabitants with a note of surprise. Dr.
Sibley wrote of a dinner party where the conversation was
dominated by the 'Vaccine Pox,' as well as how to use
charcoal to sweeten rancid butter and how to preserve
butter and beef in a warm climate. Pintard had heard
accounts of the sickly climate and dread fevers before he
came but he said, 'They laugh at our exaggerated
accounts of its being sickly.'

"Charles Gayarré, grandson of Etienne de Boré, leaves
an account of a different nature. His recollections of his
childhood on the Boré plantation, six miles above New
Orleans, give us a real glimpse of life on a sugar plantation
of the early 1800s and a firsthand account of one event of
this period that had a great impact on the economic
development of plantations.

"In 1795 Etienne de Boré successfully developed a
process to granulate sugar from cane syrup. He described
the despair of many planters when indigo production was
no longer profitable, causing a real economic dislocation.
Etienne de Boré determined to make what was considered a bold experiment in converting his plantation
from indigo to sugarcane and the production of sugar.
Despite the fears of his wife and the warnings of his friends
that failure was likely and could bring ruin, Boré per-
sisted. His first crop of sugarcane was ready for harvest in
1795. Planters watched his progress through the year with
keen interest, and suspense was great among the many
spectators who gathered around the sugar house for the

first grinding of the cane and boiling of the syrup. As they waited to see if there was success or failure, 'the stillness of death came among them,' each one holding his breath, and feeling that it was a matter of ruin or prosperity for them all. Suddenly the sugarmaker cried out in exultation, 'It granulates.' Thus a new era dawned, with the creation of the matchless delta Sugar Bowl.

"Dr. Sibley wrote in his journal in 1802 that there were fourteen sugar plantations below New Orleans, and fifty-eight above. It would be interesting to know when the fields at Magnolia Mound were converted to sugarcane. John Joyce died in 1798, three years after Boré's experiment. He was an astute businessman, so one could speculate that he was aware of the happenings downriver from his own plantation, and wonder if he was making plans to introduce cane to his own acreage. In the succession documents for Magnolia Mound at his death, tools and equipment used in indigo production are listed, but none are mentioned that have anything to do with sugarcane. From the early years of the Duplantier residency there are documents describing transactions involving the sale of cotton. So perhaps it was after the 1820s before the fields at the Mound were planted with cane.

"A French traveler to Louisiana from 1803 to 1805 took a detailed survey of the consumption of goods by the colony, with an eye toward increasing French trade here. With the advent of power-driven machines, the Industrial Revolution began first in England and resulted in her early development as a manufacturing nation. As England was able, therefore, to produce many goods cheaper, her trade dominated American imports. The Frenchman complained that fine French porcelain did not sell well, ascribing this to lack of sophisticated tastes, or possibly to the fact that it was too easily broken by slaves taking care of it. He observed that the tableware in common use was a 'nice English earthenware,' of which Leeds creamware, green Feather Edge pattern, is an example. Magnolia Mound now has an extensive collection of this pattern on display.

"Feminine fashion he noted in detail. The favored fabrics of Louisiana ladies of this period were muslin and calico, with silk used only for special occasions such as large balls. These fabrics were perfect for the climate, being light and thin, but more important, were much cheaper than the French product. However, the English calico faded with the first washing and was so thin that it tore very easily and wore out quickly. The Frenchman admitted that this was not a complete disadvantage, for the ladies could have new frocks frequently: 'the inexpensive material feeds this avid taste for novelty.' Shipments of English cloth came into New Orleans from Philadelphia about every two weeks, and the sales attracted large crowds of women. With relatively easy access to the East Coast, the newest fashions were readily available.

"English material was used for men's fashions as well. Even in the hottest season, men of this era were attired in coats with high collars and long sleeves, chins buried in triple cravats and legs sheathed in boots. Only sympathy was expressed for their 'red faces, their labored breathing and the sweat flooding the folds of their collars, a sight really painful to see.'

"Although the Baton Rouge area could be termed frontier in the early 1800s, it had decided advantages, and was certainly not isolated. Location just upriver from a large port meant that even luxury items such as liqueurs, anchovies, fruits preserved in brandy, almonds, and vermicelli, were available to those who could afford them. Peddlers plied their trade up and down the 'Coast' carrying their wares on their backs, in carts, or boats *à la cordelle*—pulled against the current by a rope thrown over the shoulders of men who walked along the levee. There was even a post between New Orleans and Natchez every two weeks, taking five days for the distance of about 240 miles. By the early 1800s, New Orleans had two newspapers, *Le Moniteur de la Louisiane,* and the *Louisiana Gazette,* established in 1804. Not until March 18, 1819, did Baton Rouge have its own paper, the Baton Rouge *Gazette,* published weekly in both French and English editions.

The Edwards article concludes "The restored Magnolia Mound is representative of the early plantations that developed in an uninterrupted succession on both sides of the Mississippi. From the eyewitness accounts we are allowed a glimpse into the past and learn something of how these inhabitants lived and what their concerns were. We can even reconstruct, perhaps, some of the topics of conversation that went on over the teacups in the parlor at Magnolia Mound."

In addition to discussing the constant political upheavals and economic problems, the Duplantiers and their friends no doubt discussed the adventures of Jean Lafitte and his band of pirates roaming the waters off the Louisiana coast, the first public schools in Point Coupee, colleges being established in New Orleans and Jackson, and a new itinerant artist working in New Orleans and the Felicianas who spent more time painting birds than portraits. Their economic woes were mollified when banks were organized to assist Louisianians with loans. They were concerned with the progress of the new sugar plantations. The French newspaper had new competition with an English one, *The Gazette,* a sure sign that the U.S. Americans were settling in. Fascinating accounts of the Lewis and Clark expedition were reported. The first steamboat chugged down the river in 1812. How many of the four thousand Baton Rouge inhabitants realized the future impact of this achievement?

The most exciting event that took place during the Duplantier years at Magnolia Mound was the visit to Baton Rouge of the Marquis de Lafayette in April of 1825.

Armand and his son accompanied the war hero from New Orleans. Fortunately there is an eyewitness account of the momentous event by Lafayette's secretary, A. Levasseur.

> Twenty-four hours after leaving New Orleans, we arrived at Duncan's Point, where we were met by a delegation of citizens who had come down from Baton Rouge, which is situated eight miles above, to ask General Lafayette to stop and spend a few moments among them. The general thankfully accepted the invitation and two hours afterward we landed at the foot of the amphitheatre above which the city is built.
>
> The landing was filled with the people of the city, at the head of whom marched the municipal guards. The first regiment of the Union was drawn up in battle array under the same star spangled banner which had previously been planted over the ruins of the Spanish despotism by the inhabitants of the parishes in the face of the greatest dangers.
>
> Accompanied by the populace and the magistrates, the general repaired to the reception Hall wherein he found the busts of Washington and Jackson crowned with laurels and flowers. In this place he received the testimonials of affection from all of the people, and went with them to the fort where the garrison awaited him. As the troops marched past him he received a salute of 24 guns.
>
> Next we went into the main room of the building in order to inspect the barracks, but to our great astonishment, we found on entering the first room, that it was not filled with beds, nor arms, nor "gay with all the accoutrements of war," but contained a numerous assembly of beautiful ladies brilliantly attired, who surrounded the general and offered him flowers and refreshments.
>
> The general was deeply touched by this agreeable surprise, and he remained for some time in the midst of the charming garrison. Upon our return to the city we met a great gathering of citizens who had joined together for the purpose of tendering a public banquet to the general, where there prevailed the candid cordiality of the French.
>
> It was almost dark when we went on board the Natchez to continue our journey.
>
> When we departed from Baton Rouge we were grieved to leave for a second time, some of the persons who had

accompanied us from New Orleans, notably, Mr. Joseph Armand Duplantier, and his son, whose tender friendship had been so helpful to the general.

Baton Rouge is situated on the left bank of the river, 137 miles above New Orleans.

The trip to that place is a very interesting one. For some miles after leaving New Orleans, the eye rests agreeably on scenes of fine sugar and cotton plantations which border the stream. They are embellished with orange groves, in the center of which are located the snow white mansions of the planters. There are avenues of oaks, cedars, and magnolias, numerous bearing pecan trees, hedges of osage orange and cherokee rose.

Little by little, the houses and gardens lessen in number, but all the way to Baton Rouge one continues to see fine lands well cultivated.

These plantations extend along the river, and reach back some times nearly a mile to the dense swamps which serve as their boundaries. The soil is composed entirely of the fertile sediment deposited by former inundations of the Mississippi, which is now confined within its bed by artificial dikes. A special law requires that each riparian proprietor keep the levee in front of his property in good condition.

Two years after Lafayette's visit Armand died. Fergus Duplantier became the executor of the financially troubled estate. Magnolia Mound plantation, at that time mortgaged, was in 1836 sold to John Dawson; however, three years later Constance repurchased it. She died in 1841 at her son Alfred's home in Beauregard Town, an area now in the city of Baton Rouge. In 1846 her heirs sold Magnolia Mound plantation and its livestock, implements, and fifty-two slaves to Alvarez Fisk and David Chambers, who did not reside in the Baton Rouge area. Thus it was what it had once been, an investment plantation operated for an absentee landlord. The act of sale notes that it was cultivated as a sugar plantation. The partners did not keep the plantation long, however, for in 1849 it was sold to George Hall and again became a family residence.

CHAPTER IV

The Enigma of a Prince

"We had a prince here once upon a time, not a visiting prince, nor a bogus prince in a menagerie, but a real live prince who lived and moved and had his being on a plantation just below town. The place is known as the Williams plantation and was bought from Mr. Duplantier by Prince Murat, the son of Caroline Bonaparte." So goes the 1918 essay for the Historical Society of East and West Baton Rouge. The author had most of the facts correct, except that the prince purchased his property from Bernard and Dubreuil Villars, who had purchased it from Fergus Duplantier. Fergus Duplantier acquired the property from part of the Constance Joyce Duplantier Magnolia Mound property.

Somehow, through the years, various writers have moved the prince to Constance Duplantier's Magnolia Mound. According to the conveyance records, when Constance Duplantier sold Magnolia Mound to John Wesley Dawson, the property was bounded below by the lands owned by the Villars. When the Villars sold their plantation to Murat on March 24, 1837, it was "bounded on the north by Dawson's property," which had been purchased from Constance Joyce Duplantier. Murat was unable to pay for Villar's plantation, so it was returned to them on January 17, 1838. (Dawson resold Magnolia Mound to Constance Duplantier in 1839.)

It is conceivable that while Dawson owned Magnolia Mound it could have been leased to Prince Murat. The Magnolia Mound research committee has searched for mid-nineteenth-century leases to no avail. The prince's residence remains a fascinating mystery, but his short sojourn in Baton Rouge resulted in Magnolia Mound's main house being called "the Prince Murat house" in the mid-twentieth century.

In 1918, when the above-quoted Historical Society article was written, the property that Murat had once owned belonged to Charles P. Williams. It was a part of the Gartness plantation eventually sold to Louisiana State University. A. J. Hanna, who wrote *A Prince in Their Midst* (1946), correctly stated that Murat owned "a sugar plantation near Baton Rouge, twenty acres of which fronting the river later became the northwestern portion of the Louisiana State University." Hanna referred to the plantation as Magnolia Mound.

Who was this prince who left a lasting impression on Baton Rouge? He was Charles Louis Napoleon Achille Murat (1801–1847), the elder son of Joachim Murat and Caroline Bonaparte, sister of Napoleon I. In 1806 he became crown prince of Naples, his father's kingdom. After Napoleon's death, Murat went to Austria and then, in 1823, he came to America. He lived in Saint Augustine, Florida, and had a plantation near Tallahassee. Murat married a widow, Catherine Willis Gray, a great-grand-niece of George Washington. Achille Murat became an American citizen and for a short while practiced law in New Orleans. He wrote three books on American life, which were published in France. Everyone who has written about the prince agrees that while in Baton Rouge he led a lavish social life, often enjoyed hunting, and was deeply in debt.

Did Murat live in the present Magnolia Mound? Or were Fergus Duplantier's plantation and house also called "Magnolia Mound" because they were acquired from part of the Magnolia Mound plantation? Was there a mistake or a misunderstanding when twentieth-century writers attempted to locate the Murat residence in Baton Rouge? One thing is certain: there was in Baton Rouge a real live prince who will be entangled forever in the history of Magnolia Mound.

PART II

CHAPTER V

⟨❄◉❄⟩

Antebellum
Plantation Life

By the 1840s Baton Rouge had become a major river port between New Orleans and Natchez, serving as a supply base for the plantations on both sides of the Mississippi River. In 1846 the Louisiana legislature voted to move the state capital from New Orleans to Baton Rouge. A site overlooking the river was selected, and in November construction of the new statehouse, designed by New Orleans architect James Dakin, was begun. Work on this architectural extravaganza, which still stands, was completed in 1849. As the town became the seat of state government, more people from all over the state, including legislators and businessmen, visited the growing community. In 1850 there were about 4,000 persons living in the Baton Rouge area, of whom about 2,500 were white, over 1,000 were slaves, and about 250 were free Negroes.

The commercial life of the town was centered near the Mississippi River. Close to the levee one could find dry-goods and clothing stores, general stores, drugstores, a bookstore, and several hotels and coffeehouses. The Mississippi River linked Baton Rouge with other parts of the state and other sections of the country. Steamboats called the "regulars" brought needed materials and supplies to the merchants, and mail, newspapers, and visitors to the residents of the town. These steamboats stopped each week, trading between Baton Rouge, New Orleans, and Bayou Sara. There were also ferryboats that traveled between Baton Rouge and West Baton Rouge Parish. The people of Baton Rouge also depended largely upon the river for their transportation; roads were generally poor, and railroads were not to be developed until the 1880s. Although rail service between Baton Rouge and Grosse Tete was available as early as 1857, this small enterprise ended with the Civil War.

After Baton Rouge became the state capital, interest in state politics increased. Political issues on the local, state, and national levels were often topics of conversation. Two newspapers in town offered varying political views: the Baton Rouge *Gazette* supported the Whigs, whereas the *Democratic Advocate* presented the Democrats' point of view. Newspapers and magazines from other parts of the country provided Baton Rougeans with differing attitudes on the slavery issue and informed them of various sectional demands coming from the Northeast, West, and South. Disagreements throughout the country on the slavery issue came to the fore during the Missouri crisis, from 1819 to 1821, and grew stronger with each succeeding decade.

But politics and slavery were not the only subjects that were discussed at the coffeehouses or over dinner wine. Crops, the weather, and the subtle changes of season were dealt with in detail. Talk often centered on the Mississippi, the river upon which the planters depended for their livelihood, which also could cause loss of life and property during spring floods.

As hard as these Baton Rouge folk worked, so did they seek recreation. The warm climate permitted them to pursue the pleasures of the out-of-doors almost year round; these activities included hunting, fishing, and horseback riding. Many Baton Rougeans traveled regularly to New Orleans on the river. A fascinating show-place often referred to simply as "the city," New Orleans offered such cultural attractions as opera, ballet, and concerts. Closer to home, there was a great deal of visiting between plantations. Residents would go to see friends or relatives and, due to the poor roads and other transporta-tion difficulties, would always plan to stay several days or even weeks. These visits would provide their hosts with excuses for social gatherings. Neighbors would be invited for parties and dances, and dinners with conversation after the meals would last far into the night.

For entertainment in Baton Rouge, people went to dances and balls or attended lectures, musicals, school programs, or political rallies. Picnics, barbeques, and boat rides were popular, as were the circuses, fairs, and shows that came to town. Those who enjoyed horse racing could attend the races at Magnolia Race Track, which opened in 1847. The Protestant and Roman Catholic churches provided various social outings as well.

Into this small and prosperous community George Otis Hall and his wife Emma moved in 1849 (figures 7 and 8). On Wednesday, February 28, of that year, George Hall purchased Magnolia Mound plantation in an auction from Alvarez Fiske and David Chambers for a price of $79,710.50, which included fifty-five slaves. Hall was to own this property for twenty years, a time span that would see tumultuous changes in the life of the plantation and the South.

George Otis Hall was born in 1809 in Charleston, South Carolina, the fourth of seventeen children. His parents were William Hall of Scotland and Hannah Jacks Hall from Charleston. From research done by LaVerne Thomas III, we know that in 1815 George Hall went to England to live, where he probably obtained his educa-tion. He later returned to the United States and came to

Figure 7. George Otis Hall owned Magnolia Mound from 1849 to 1869.

New Orleans sometime in the mid 1830s, for he was listed in the New Orleans city directory in 1838.

In 1840 Hall was Cashier at the Commercial Bank of New Orleans. At this time he shared a house with Amaron

Figure 8. Emma LeDoux Hall, wife of George Hall.

LeDoux, his business partner, and LeDoux's young nephew, Auguste Provosty.

Hall made the first of several purchases of land in 1839 with his partners Amaron LeDoux and Alphonse Milten-berger. The thirty-two-hundred-acre tract was located on the Mississippi River at Raccourri Bend in Pointe Coupee Parish, and was acquired for $25,000. It later became known as "Normandy," one of the great sugar plantations of the area.

Amaron LeDoux's niece was Charlotte Emma LeDoux, described in an early letter as "a great 'belle' in the ball-rooms of New Orleans." Emma, born in 1825 to Zenon LeDoux, Jr., and Mathilde Vignes LeDoux, was the fourth of eight children. Hall married her at her father's home in Pointe Coupee in 1845. A marriage contract between George and Emma gave details of Hall's financial holdings, listing not only the plantation at Raccourri, but also a parcel of land in Terrebonne parish, one-third interest in the firm of LeDoux and Company, a house in Charleston, and land in Illinois. He gave a gift of $10,000 to Emma, as well as all of his furnishings and silverware in New Orleans, which he estimated at $1,800. Emma declared in the contract that her wardrobe, jewelry, and other personal belongings were valued at $1,200.

LaVerne Thomas's research continues the story. "The couple returned to their life in New Orleans for a time, and the couple's first child [George William] was born in their home on Canal Street. Then, in 1847 began the first of several voyages abroad, and the second child [Mathilde Alice] was born in Vienna, Austria, at the home of the American Ambassador. Hall, however, was searching for the proper plantation on which to rear his family, and by 1849 he had found it." Five other children were born to the Halls while they lived at Magnolia Mound: Emma Natalie was born in March of 1849, one month after Hall's purchase of the plantation, Lawrence Otis was born in 1850, Oliver Otis, in 1851, Robert Cunningham, in 1853, Henry Maurice in 1855, and Frederic Durive, in 1858. (The four remaining children, Francis, Caroline Adelaide Marie Virginie, Alice Marie, and Marie Louise, were born after 1861 and would not know Magnolia Mound as their home.)

Magnolia Mound was a working sugar plantation when George Otis Hall bought it. The 1860 census shows that Hall had seventy-nine slaves and twenty-one dwellings on the plantation, and that 173,000 pounds of sugarcane had been produced. (Cotton is not listed at this time as being a crop on the place.)

From research done by Cynthia Cash, an article by Alton Moody entitled "Slavery on Louisiana Sugar Plantations," letters written by members of the Hall family, and other sources, we are able to put together a good picture of how the Halls must have lived before the Civil War. A painting of the plantation (figure 9) shows us what Magnolia Mound may have looked like when Hall owned it. The original of this painting is owned by a Hall descendant who lives in France.

The plantation's layout was typical of many sugar plantations located on the Mississippi River. The main house, or "big house," stood apart from the other buildings, and was located on a natural ridge. A road on the side of the house went from the river landing straight back to the sugar house. The overseer's house was located near the "big house," and several rows of slave houses were arranged in lines on either side of the road leading to the sugar house. Many other structures were located on the plantation, including outbuildings such as the barns, stables, poultry houses, *pigeonnieres,* tool shed, blacksmith shop, and storage sheds.

The sugar house, the operational center of the plantation, was built equidistant from the levee crest and the swamp. It was therefore near the swamp, from where the wood was hauled, near the cane fields, and near the river, where the crop was shipped. Magnolia Mound's sugar house was located where the Blundon Home Orphanage now stands. It is said that the first building on the orphanage grounds was built on the foundation of the sugar house.

The sugar house was a two-story brick structure with a qrinding mill, cane juice clarifier, boiling apparatus, crystallizing trough, and purging facilities. The first grinding mills were driven by horses or oxen; steam mills were not introduced to Louisiana until 1822. Although many small plantations continued to use animal power even in the late 1800s because they could not afford the expensive steam mills, we know from a letter written to

Figure 9. This river-view painting of the house and grounds of Magnolia Mound Plantation, made during George Hall's period of ownership, is now in the possession of family descendants in France.

Hall from his overseer that Magnolia Mound had a steam mill.

The slaves' houses, also called "quarter houses," were built of wood and had cypress-shingled roofs. From research done by John Rehder on Louisiana sugar plantations, we can speculate that the Magnolia Mound quarter houses were probably of Creole design, raised off the ground by brick piers, with a built-in front porch created by the roof overhang, a central chimney, and double front doors. These houses often had two main living areas, one behind each of the two front doors. Sometimes two families occupied one house, with one family living and sleeping in each of the two separate one-room living areas. Outdoor privies, vegetable plots, and pig or chicken pens were usually located behind the cabins.

The overseer's house was the same type as the quarter houses, but larger and neater, reflecting the difference in position between the overseer and the field hands. The overseer's house that is open for viewing at Magnolia Mound was moved onto its present site in 1977. Its original location near the sugar house eventually became Vermont Street as the city grew around it. This particular house was probably built in the latter part of the nineteenth century, perhaps as far back as 1870. The house that served as the overseer's house before this time is believed to have been destroyed during the Civil War. The significance of the present overseer's house is not so much its age but the fact that it is the only remaining dependency or outbuilding of Magnolia Mound plantation.

George Hall's agricultural responsibilities revolved around his sugarcane crop. The cane was planted from January until March and then was cultivated from March until the first of July. After the crop had been "laid by," Hall began directing general work on the plantation: sowing hay, gathering corn, cutting and hauling wood, making brick, repairing the sugar house machinery, and preparing for the grinding season. Grinding of the cane began in October and lasted until about the end of December. During this grueling season almost every available worker, including Hall and his overseer, worked eighteen hours a day for weeks at a time. Extra food, flour, and coffee were often given to the slaves to sustain them during this demanding time and to increase their good will.

Although the sugarcane crop demanded the major part of Hall's time, many other duties also required his supervision. Corn, peas, and potatoes were cultivated, bridges had to be repaired, and the levees had to be mended and carefully maintained during the spring flood season. Hall's concern over the flooding of the river is expressed in a letter he wrote to his son George in 1858.

> The Mississippi river has been unusually high this year and has overflowed its banks in many places, inundating the country for hundreds of miles, on both sides and doing great damage to the crops of Cotton, Cane, and Corn. For-

tunately I have sustained no injury whatever. From St. James down to the Balize nearly every Plantation on that side is under water, including the Armands; and Doctor Wiendahl's—this you will be sorry to learn. The view of the mighty waters, as they sweep along in front of us, is indescribably grand and as you may suppose, we have been living in fear and trembling. They are now receding in the upper country—some 700 miles above us—and we may hope soon to see them within their ordinary channels.

A large work force was necessary for the smooth running of Magnolia Mound as a sugar plantation. The Halls owned a number of slaves, some who worked as house servants, some as general field laborers, and others who contributed work that required special skills—the sugar makers, shoemakers, brickmakers, wagonmakers, blacksmiths, mechanics, coopers, carpenters, tanners, ox- and mule-drivers, millers, and cooks. We can assume that Hall treated his slaves fairly and enjoyed a good relationship with them, because most of them chose to remain on the plantation after the Civil War.

Some details on the slaves' daily life, their houses, and their food and clothes are described in Alton Moody's article, "Slavery on Louisiana Sugar Plantations." This helps us to know how the slaves probably lived at Magnolia Mound.

The slave cabins were of simple construction. The windows had no glass, but there were shutters to close at mealtimes and at night to ensure privacy. The slaves cooked at their cabin fireplaces at night. Extra clothes were hung on pegs on the wall, and their simple furniture included crude beds with mattresses made of moss, straw, or grass.

Slaves on sugar plantations were fed at least as well, if not better, than those in other regions. They were given substantial amounts of food in order to maintain their health and to enable them to perform their labor efficiently. Salt pork, cornbread, and molasses were the mainstay of their diet, with vegetables added from their own gardens or from the kitchen garden. The house slaves usually ate at the "big kitchen" at breakfast. The field hands, however, were sent out to work before sunrise, and their breakfast was taken out to them about 8:00 A.M. All of the plantation's workers ate at the plantation kitchen at noon.

It was necessary for everyone to drink cistern water to avoid disease; drinking stagnant water often caused cholera. The low land and marshes in Louisiana made this a special problem. In 1849 and 1850 there were serious outbreaks of cholera.

Fevers, lung trouble, hookworm, yellow fever, and other illnesses afflicted residents of the slave cabins and the "big house" as well. When a slave became ill, he was cared for by Hall, his wife, and the overseer. Hall probably had a doctor on retainer who would come to look after those with serious illnesses. For less severe sicknesses the slaves often preferred to use their own remedies and methods of treatment. Slaves who were no longer able to work because of illness, injury, or advanced age were allowed to stay on the plantation and were cared for.

Hall and his wife were also responsible for the clothing needs of their slaves. Some clothes were "store bought," but most were made on the plantation under Emma Hall's supervision. In the spring and in the fall the men were usually given a pair of pants, a shirt, a hat, and a pair of shoes; in the winter, wool coats, jackets, and blankets were given out. Waterproof sacks were used to keep clothing dry during the rainy seasons. At Christmas, Hall and his wife gave the slaves other articles of clothing as presents.

Everyone looked forward to rest days and holidays. The slaves were usually given Saturday afternoons and Sundays off. Sometimes there was a holiday on the day grinding season ended, and the slaves would form a procession and go up to the big house for a drink, perhaps having a dance afterward. They also celebrated holidays at Christmas and New Year's. At Magnolia Mound on New

Year's Day, the Negroes brought gifts to the master. In a letter to his wife written in January of 1861, George Hall gives this account: "I drank to your health on New Year's Day. The Negroes again brought gifts and I am rich in good things, particularly eggs and fowl! Game is very abundant, and I enjoy eating two woodcocks each day for my dinner. The hedges and garden are full of partridges and I enjoy hunting them. . . ."

Weddings were another fine opportunity for celebrations. In the twenty-five to fifty years preceding the Civil War, slaves set up family groups, a couple living as man and wife, with or without a religious marriage ceremony. Some form of ceremony usually took place, however, even if it was merely "jumping over the broomstick." (This southern Negro custom dates back to the late eighteenth century. To symbolize their union, both the man and the woman would jump over a broomstick.)

By the time the Hall family lived at Magnolia Mound, weddings among the slaves were probably religious in nature. Church was held on the plantation, and slaves were encouraged to attend. We can assume that they were instructed in the Roman Catholic faith, as Emma Hall and the children were Catholic. George Hall, being from South Carolina and of Scottish descent, might not have been born Catholic.

The personal life of the overseer differed greatly from that of the typical slave. We know from Hall's letters that he had several different overseers during the period that he owned Magnolia Mound. In January, 1861, George Hall wrote to his wife, who was visiting family in Europe (this letter is translated from French).

> My dear Emma,
>   Your letter, along with that of the children, just arrived. I thank you for it. It gives me such pleasure to know that you are all well. I wrote you eight or ten days ago; since then we have had terrible weather, rain every day and at the moment there is a fog which would make London proud.

One can barely see the columns on the gallery and everything in the house is damp and uncomfortably warm.
There are at least ten steamboats lost in the fog across from
the house, and their whistles are making enough noise to
deafen the world. We are making little progress with the
cane planting. The new steward [foreman] has arrived. The
other left some time ago with his interesting family, and he
now has time to become drunk whenever he feels like it.
The new one, they say, is very organized and he seems like
a good enough fellow, but I'm afraid that he is weak of
character. But we'll see.

The position of the overseer of the plantation was not to
be envied. Although, unlike the plantation owner, the
overseer typically had little education, it was upon his
shoulders that the success of the plantation rested. The
overseer was responsible for the welfare, physical care,
and discipline of the slaves, the care of the livestock and
farm equipment, and the production of the crops. He was
in charge of work gangs and supervised the field laborers.
Another of his duties was to keep a plantation book, in
which he recorded the births, deaths, illnesses, and daily
work rates of all the slaves. He also kept up with crop-
production figures and other matters relating to plantation business. In addition, he was depended upon to keep
the plantation safe and secure.

Although his role on the plantation was a vital one, he
lived in a social vacuum. He was forbidden to associate
with the slaves, was usually discouraged from entertaining friends of his own, and was asked not to leave the
plantation except on plantation business. Kate Stone
describes the overseer's status in her book *Brokenburn*.

Altogether it was a difficult position to fill satisfactorily. The
men were a coarse, uncultivated class, knowing little more
than to read and write. . . . Neither they nor their families
were ever invited to any of the entertainment given by the
planters, except some large function, such as a wedding
given at the home of the employer. If they came, they did
not expect to be introduced to the guests but were
expected to amuse themselves, watching the crowd. They

visited only among themselves, except an occasional call
of the wife and children on the family of the employer. . . .
Of course in case of sickness at the overseer's, the lady at
the great house saw that they were not neglected and that
they were well waited on. There was always a woman furnished to wait on the overseer's family, and if he had many
children, a half-grown girl was furnished to nurse. There
was often kindest relations existing between the two
families until the overseer would leave or be discharged;
then they would drop entirely out of each other's lives.

Although this profession has been much maligned, with
special thanks to Harriet Beecher Stowe, research
indicates that most southern overseers performed their
duties in a competent manner. Given the circumstances of
employment, it is easy to understand why they often did
not remain at any one plantation for long.

The lives of George and Emma Hall contrasted sharply
with those of the slaves and overseer. Although they
worked hard as owners of a large working plantation, they
also enjoyed certain luxuries. They were attended by a
number of house servants, including housekeeper, nurse,
cook, and body servants. As the children became older,
they had slave children assigned to serve them and be
their companions. George Hall had family members living
in England, and Emma had relatives living in France; they
often traveled abroad to visit.

At Magnolia Mound Hall's day began early, taking
advantage of the natural light. His morning probably
started with an early morning cup of coffee served in the
bedroom or on the back gallery. Breakfast was served
several hours later. He spent his days making sure that the
plantation ran smoothly and efficiently. In addition to
working with his overseer and slaves, he spent a good deal
of time on the road, going into Baton Rouge and down the
river to New Orleans, attending to plantation business,
marketing, and the shipping of his sugarcane crop.

Emma Hall's days were filled with a variety of duties. It
was she who organized and planned food preparation,

supervised the housework, managed the tending of the gardens, saw to the clothing, health, and religious instruction of the slaves, and cared for her family. We can be sure that taking care of the children consumed a large portion of her day. Early education of the children was usually conducted in the home by the mother; we know that for a time at Magnolia Mound, a governess helped with the lessons. As the children grew older, they were sent away to school for their formal education. The girls were sent to a Catholic school in St. James Parish, and the boys were sent abroad.

George William, the Halls' oldest son, was sent to England to school at Stonyhurst in 1857, when he was twelve years old. The Halls' large family was closely knit and filled with affection, and this is shown in several letters written to George while he was away at school. Mathilde, George's ten-year-old sister, wrote this charming letter on July 25, 1857.

> My dear Brother,
>   I hope that you are well and that you have had a happy voyage. Mama received your letter which you wrote from South West pass, we all were very glad to hear good news from you, and I hope dear Brother that we will continue to do so.
>   I have taken good care of your little garden, and it is very pretty. I planted some pine apples and many other things in it. Mama has three mocking birds for you, they are almost raised and are very pretty too. I have not much news to tell you dear brother, every thing is the same here. Papa saw in the papers that your ship was spoken, when you were four days at Sea—we were very glad.
>   We are all well. We have school every day, Miss is our teacher. The next letter you receive from me will be in french and you will see how I am improved. Do not be too long before you answer My letter, dear Brother.
>   Papa, Mama and all the children and Miss send you a kiss.

Our love to Aunt Alice and to our uncles and aunts. Tell aunt Alice, that altho I do not remember her, I love her very much.

Adieu, my dear brother, your affectionate Sister,

MATHILDE

Little Boubou tells you *dits.*

You will be sorry that poor Tom, the old carriage horse, who took us to school so often, died yesterday.

Two letters written by George Hall to his son center on school and hard work. Parents of today can easily identify with his concern over his son's education.

September 30, 1857

My dear Son,

... You are now, I trust, at Stonyhurst, bravely at work at your studies, determined to learn as much as you can and make up for lost time. I wrote early in August to the President of the College and hope soon to hear from him with a favorable account of you. I need not say, my dear son, that I fully expect you to be as attentive as you can, to all your duties, obedient to your Instructors, careful with your books and clothes, and that whatever you undertake to learn, you will *learn well.* You have now an excellent opportunity to learn and should profit by it. You can have little idea, too, of the pleasure and happiness it will afford to your Mother and to me to receive accounts of your good conduct in all respects.

Your mother who was unwell when you left, is now much better. She is sitting in the parlour with the children, who are all the picture of good health and are just now engaged with their books and slates. Mathilde has taken your place and overlooks them. Lawrence and Otis take lessons on the piano, little Robert begins to write and even little *Boubou* is trying what he can do with his pencil—he is the same amusing little fellow, always in good humor—he rides up and down the piazza on my walking cane and says he is "going to see Willy." They, with your Mama, all send you their love. Mathilde would write to you, but she says you have yet taken no notice of her letter and she will wait until she receives your reply. I hope that in future we will receive letters from you regularly. We shall be glad to hear all about the College, your studies and the books you read. I suppose you are a subscriber to the Library. I enclose a letter sent to us for you from Aunt Armantine. As I requested you will write to your Mother in french and to me in English. Do not forget to read french books and to speak it every opportunity you have.

I find that my paper is out and will therefore bid you adieu. God bless you my George.

Your affectionate,
FATHER

July 5, 1858

My dear George,

I have received and have to thank you for your letter of 23rd May. We were happy to learn by it that you continue in good health and also that you believe yourself to be progressing in your studies, which I hope to be really the case and which certainly will be if you desire it and are attentive and *industrious*. Almost anything, my son, can be attained by a resolute determination and industry. You recollect the difficulty and trouble you used to have in making your traps and cages and in protecting your mocking birds and red birds from their enemies—the dogs and cats—but at last you succeeded and you and I inscribed upon your cages the motto: *labor omnis vincit*, which I hope you will never forget.

Your Mama also received a letter from you lately in french. She left a few days ago on a short visit to the Point, with Mathilde, Lawrence, Otis and little Boubou and I am left at home with Cissy and Robert. They are well and pass their time pretty much as they used to do. Mr. and Mrs. Dursive came up with the children lately and stayed a fortnight with us, to the great delight of the little folks, as you may suppose, but they all regretted that you were not here to join in their frolics.

We are sorry to learn by your letter that your Aunt Alice has been so unwell. We have not heard from her, or from your uncles for a very long time. We had been in hopes to have visited them and you this summer, but you have such a lot of little brothers and sisters that it is difficult either to leave them or to move about with them. We will soon be able to send three or four of them to school and it will then be an easier matter. Lawrence and Otis are nearly old enough now, but we are undecided where to send them. One of my friends, who has his children there, recommends Dresden and another Geneva. . . . You ought to learn Italian—it is very easy. I studied it for a few months and managed to speak it currently. It is besides the first language that you uttered and in Rome, tho you were then a very little fellow, you have often shouted with the multitude: *viva pio hone.* You ought also, by and by, to take lessons in dancing and fencing. Let me know always your wishes in these matters. . . .

Write to us often and *long* letters. You see I have set you the example. Your Mama will write to you on her return home. The children join me in best love to you. God bless you my dear George.

Your affectionate
Father

We are expecting a visit from Judge Gayarre—he and Mrs. G. often inquire about you.

In 1859, Mathilde and Emma were sent to school in St. James Parish. Mathilde was twelve, and Emma was ten years old. We have a letter written in French to Mathilde from her mother, January 16, 1860.

Dear Mathilde,

I just returned from the Point yesterday on the train. I was there for Mix's wedding which took place last Wednesday. She looked lovely in her wedding veil. There were lots of people and the young ladies and young men danced until midnight. Aunts Armantine, Celeste, and Adele were the maids of honor. They were sorry that you and Emma were not there for the ceremony. I was happy to learn from your last letter, dear daughter, that you are well. I hope to find you in magnificent health when I come to see you, which I will do as soon as I am able. Don't be too impatient, for you know that I have many children and am not able to leave when I wish.

I received a letter from Aunt Clo today. She told me that
Anne had been very ill with a bad cold but that she is fine
now.

Boubou was delighted with his little note; he holds it very
carefully—he and the others are very well and ask me to
send you a kiss. Your papa is well as always and spends his
time comfortably, he also sends you a kiss. Lastly, we have
had no news from your brother.

Good-bye dear child. I send everyone's love. Give my
regards to the Ladies.

Your loving mother,
E. H<small>ALL</small>

Later that year, Mathilde and Emma were taken out of
school so that they could travel abroad with their parents
and the other children. George Hall returned to Magnolia
Mound for the grinding season, but Emma and the
children remained in England.

In that same year Abraham Lincoln was elected president of the United States. He was a member of the newly
formed antislavery Republican Party, and as such his
name was not even listed on the ballots in Baton Rouge or
elsewhere in the Deep South. South Carolina voted in
December to leave the Union, and Mississippi, Florida,
Georgia, and Alabama followed suit. In Louisiana,
Governor Thomas O. Moore called for a special session of
the legislature to take place on December 10 in Baton
Rouge. At that time the state legislators decided to hold a
state convention in January of 1861 to determine
whether Louisiana would secede from the Union. This
tense political situation was echoed in George Hall's letter
to his wife in England, written in French, on January 8,
1861. Hall's secessionist attitude can be easily under-
stood when we remember his South Carolina background.

My dear Emma,
   . . . You will notice from the newspapers that political
affairs have become more and more entangled and God
knows how all this will end. I think there will be a con-

federation of the Southern States. *There is no one* here who would not desire the separation; it is unanimous. We want to be governed by laws and not by madmen and preachers—the latter who know *nothing of life,* are now and always will be imbeciles in the practical and political affairs of human life. You see a great deal on the subject of all this *in the newspapers* but one hardly notices it; all is calm and working here in Louisiana, in spite of the fact that there is too much liberty or rather license in the country, everyone votes, foreigner as well as native, and as the ignorant and vicious are always in the majority in any country, in ours as well as others, one cannot expect anything else. If this right of universal suffrage continues much longer, a general division of wealth will be voted in as the socialists would like to do in France and as will be done in England if one listens to the absurdities of Lord John Russell, and the result will be that there will be no more civilization except in the countries which we call despotic but which we should call law abiding. The rabble is never able to govern with justice nor to respect the rights of people or property. But enough of politics. I believe that England and the other European countries will profit by what is taking place in the United States. Too much liberty ruins civilization. Alice asks my opinion about what is happening here. You may tell her what I've told you in the preceding and tell her that the only part of the United States which remains civilized is South Carolina because *it has always* kept its old laws—no one votes who does not pay taxes on his property—foreigners and those who own nothing have never voted in this state because they have no interest in the country and they have always resisted *ideal* systems of government. There, *gentlemen* govern the rabble and they find this more sensible than being governed by them.

I have nothing new to tell you. I have not left the house since my return from the city and I have seen no one. I will go to the city again in several days to try to sell crops. Prices have fallen to nothing. . . .

I will write to you from town. Perhaps I will go to the Point before going to town—but the weather is so bad. Good-bye, my dear Emma. I send you a kiss. I am writing in haste.
GEORGE

Hall's prediction of a unanimous vote was not fulfilled, for many Louisianians were moderates who wished to wait and see what Lincoln's presidency would bring. There were enough who shared Hall's convictions, however, to carry the vote for secession on January 26, 1861.

CHAPTER VI

Civil War
and Reconstruction

After the January vote in favor of secession from the Union, Louisiana was an independent republic for two months, becoming a member of the Confederate States in March of 1861. The Civil War began on April 12, and Baton Rougeans volunteered to fight in a war that they believed would soon end. By June more than half of the thirteen hundred registered voters in town had enlisted. The ladies saw their sweethearts, husbands, brothers, and sons off to war with kisses, tears, and fluttering handkerchiefs. Bands played, and the "stars and bars" was flown everywhere. Soon the sounds of music would fade into memory.

George Otis Hall was too old to enlist to fight for the cause he felt to be so just. He left in 1861 to rejoin his wife and children in Europe. He remained in England and France until 1865, when he returned to Baton Rouge to assess the damage done to his plantation during the war. From 1861 until the war's end, Magnolia Mound was left in the hands of Hall's overseer.

Baton Rouge was not to remain part of the Confederacy for very long. Federal forces headed for New Orleans in April of 1862, and Louisiana's Governor Thomas O. Moore ordered that the state capital be moved from Baton

Rouge to Opelousas. Soon afterward it was moved again to Shreveport, where it remained until the war was over. Moore also ordered that cotton and other crops be destroyed to keep them from Federal troops. On April 26 in Baton Rouge hundreds of bales of cotton were set on fire and sent floating down the river to New Orleans. Sarah Morgan Dawson, author of A Confederate Girl's Diary, was a witness to this event.

> We went this morning to see the cotton burning—a sight never before witnessed, and probably never again to be seen. Wagons, drays—everything that can be driven or rolled—were loaded with the bales and taken a few squares back to burn on the commons. Negroes were running around, cutting them open, piling them up, and setting them afire. All were as busy as though their salvation depended upon disappointing the Yankees. Later, Charlie sent for us to come to the river and see him fire a flatboat loaded with the precious material for which the Yankees are risking their bodies and souls. . . . There, piled the length of the whole levee, or burning in the river, lay the work of thousands of negroes for more than a year past. It had come from every side. Men stood by who owned the cotton that was burning or waiting to burn. They either helped, or looked on cheerfully.

New Orleans fell on April 26 and became an "occupied city" on May 1, 1862. A week later the Federal gunboat Iroquois sailed by Magnolia Mound. Commander James Palmer and a small party of men took possession of the Pentagon Barracks and the nearby arsenal without resistance. It was not until May 28 that the first shelling of Baton Rouge began, when a band of guerrillas fired upon a rowboat belonging to the U.S.S. Hartford. In retaliation the Hartford and another warship began bombarding the town. Houses near the river were severely damaged, and the terrified citizens fled their homes in panic. Hundreds headed out of town with no food or possessions, most going toward Greenwell Springs, where many residents of Baton Rouge had summer cottages. The majority of people eventually returned to their homes. The following day Brigadier General Thomas Williams and his troops came into Baton Rouge; Federal occupation of the town had begun.

The summer was unusually hot, even for Baton Rouge. Williams, a harsh taskmaster, drilled his troops in full equipment. Many of his troops were unused to the extreme heat and became ill. Rumors flew through the town that the Confederates were coming from Vicksburg to capture Baton Rouge, and in early August the long-awaited battle took place. The Confederate troops, about twenty-six hundred strong, were led by Major General John C. Breckinridge. At dawn on August 5 he attacked, certain that his troops would be protected by the Confederate ironclad *Arkansas*, which would provide artillery support against the Federal warships that were near the town. Although Breckinridge did temporarily take the town, he was forced to withdraw, for the *Arkansas* never arrived. The ship developed engine trouble a few miles above Baton Rouge and had to be destroyed by her crew. The Battle of Baton Rouge ended the day it began, with a toll of 456 Confederate forces killed or wounded. The Federals lost 383 men, including General Williams. His replacement, General Halbert Pierce, came up from New Orleans the following day, and in preparation for another Confederate attack, he ordered that all buildings between the arsenal and the river be destroyed. In all, about one-third of the town was burned. In addition, hundreds of trees were cut down to build barricades.

There was no Confederate attack, but by this time Baton Rouge was no more than a shell of a town. Troops evacuated Baton Rouge on August 21, plundering and shelling buildings as they left. The people of the town had fled during the battle of August 5, and those who returned found their homes ravaged or destroyed. Many left the devastated town and did not return until the war's end. For the inhabitants of Baton Rouge this was a time of desperation, tragedy, and heartbreak. No one had remained untouched by the events of the past four months.

The Federal troops soon returned, and their numbers were increased to seven thousand men. Magnolia Mound became occupied by Federal forces in late 1862. This letter from George Hall's overseer details the events of the occupation of the plantation:

Magnolia Mound Plantation
Jan. 15, 1865

Mr. G. O. Hall
Dear Sir   When the United States Army arived in Baton Rouge about the 17th of Sept 1862 your plantation was in good order   all the fensis & bridges together with shugur house was in good repair. Said fensis halve ben torn down & burnt by the army and negrows that was quartered on the place by the federal authoritys together with bridges and all the timbers of the shugur house except part of the coolir and 6 of juseboxes. Dec. 20, 1862 took bay horse mine and broke open the hinges of the shugur house and took out a quantity of shugur & molasses which they continued to do dayly untill the shugur and molasses was removed from the place. Dec 23rd took tin mules 2 wagons & 2 small carts & ten sets of harness. they was taken by the quarter master of the 4 Volunteers. a receipt for the same is in the hands of W. H. H. Witheril of New Orleans. Dec 25th took the following described cattle 1 bull 5 milk cows and calves 1 two year old heiffer 12 hed in all. Jan 4th 1863 to. [took] 4 wagon loads of hay & six wagon loads of corn. Jan 18th 1863 quartered 4 or 5 hundred negrows in the quarters & shugur house. At the time they put the negrows in the shugur house it was in complete order. the negrows broke the engine stole all the pipes & broke down the cane cases & burnt the slats together with 37 shugur hhds. Jan 19th, 1863 broke open the tool house & took 20 spaids 20 long handles & 10 short handled shuvels & 7 wheel barrows & 2 plows & 27 cane hoes. said negrows remained on the place until about the 20 of March 1863 when they was removed by order of the government authority about the 24th of March 1863 by order of Maj Gen Auger. there was a brigade of troops quartered on the place. It was the first brigade of Emmy's Division under the command of Col Ingraham then act Brig Gen. they took pirsession of the stable & used the

upper florering for thir tents & before they left all the stalls
& traws were broken down & made way with

Yours respetfuly
W. J. Pierce

George Hall returned to Baton Rouge in January of
1865. The following letter written to his wife eloquently
describes the condition in which he found Magnolia
Mound and Baton Rouge. He mentions in this letter the
"smoked and rent" towers of the statehouse. During the
second occupation of Baton Rouge, the statehouse was
occupied by Union troops and Confederate prisoners.
Late in December, 1862, a fire broke out, and only the
outer walls of the building were left standing. It was rebuilt
in the 1880s.

New Orleans—January 19, 1865

My dear Emma,

... I thought it best to go up at once to Baton Rouge and
obtain a pass. My former overseer and Mr. Nelson had just
arrived and went up with me—we landed on the 2nd day
after midnight, wet and cold—the hotels full and crowded,
not a sopha to be had, and I got shelter in a room with
several soldiers, and slept pretty well. On getting out in the
morning, I made my way thro' crowds of soldiers and
found our old friend Mr. Bonnecaze—who is French
consul. John had heard of my arrival and awaited me with
a joyful countenance—followed soon after by Hannibal.
After breakfast I drove down to the place, the hills in the
rear & on our upper side line from "Cherokee hill," white
with the tents of the soldiers, as far as could be seen, and as
the trees that I had taken such care of, had been all cut
down, the view in that direction was unobstructed. In front
of the river road, long lines of military waggons extending
miles below, were hauling wood for the troops. On
approaching by the avenue in front, the gate and fences
gone, but the oaks have been spared excepting a few, and
the old house amidst the trees and evergreens on the hill,
looked in the distance almost as we had left it. Of the
gardens and hedges below, scarcely a vestige remains, but
around the dwelling, the live oaks and laurels and
magnolias as luxuriant as ever and even some of the

shrubs, the myrtles, sweet olives and camellias in bloom. The hedges mostly broken and trampled down. Old Jessy and William it seems had expected me and had trimmed a little and cleaned the walk in front and from the gallery the peeks thro' the trees of the river and surrounding country were beautiful—the smoked and rent towers of the State-house in the distance. The mocking birds and cardinals singing and chirping as of old—they seem to be unconscious of the sad events and change since we had left. The place is now just within the military lines and the cavalry pickets are stationed at short distances all along the roads and fields with their carbines on their arms as if expecting an attack. Two gunboats at anchor, but with steam up, in front just opposite where the white gate stood—our old landing place on the river. The prospect is very much as it was, the sugar houses on the opposite shore are still there, but the large house of Noland Stewart is wanting—it was burnt down and the trees around it. There is not a panel of fencing left on the place, the soldiers even now, and there are 12,000 still here including cavalry, take everything within their reach for fuel. All our buildings are standing the shot and shells from the gun-boats during the battle. Bombardments fell mostly in the background, making havoc among the trees and some exploded in the pasture below the stable making huge holes in the ground. None of the people were injured, tho "Big Tom" was subsequently shot thro' the thigh and "little Tom" had his hand shattered by a ball. None of the grown hands have died since we left, save old Jane and little Sarah. You will regret the former, she was faithful to the "last" and it was she who saved our plate, with the aid of some of the others and buried it—you will be surprised to learn that there is not a piece missing. But you will be curious to know as to the household effects. In the old parlor the carpet had just been taken up and the India matting below was clean—the chairs, sophas, mirrors and tables in their places—some of the paintings on the walls, where we left them—some absent. Buttoni's Madonna, . . . Sheep, Reynold's Fruit Girl, . . . and the Dog and Cat—I greeted them with pleasure. The mosaic table and the young Augustus are intact—the latter detached from the pedestal to keep a door open—then to the dining room. Here was desolation, the two sideboards—everything smashed to pieces and everything broken. The soldiers had been thirsty and I pardoned them for what they had spared—two or three paintings still on the walls—Watteau's sleighing scene (which belongs to Mathilde) among them. All the armoires and bureaus in the rooms had been wrenched open and contents gone—my writing desk and your rosewood box also—not a remnant left of table or bed linen, glasses or china, and I had to borrow the "needful" from the overseer's wife. More than half my books are gone, but I am thankful for what is left—some seven or eight hundred volumes, scattered about—many of the sets broken. There was not a bottle of wine left in the cellar, not a horse, nor a cow and only five of the fifty odd mules left. Two families—those of the overseer and of Mr. Nelson, with their children, reside in the house—your bedroom is the parlour of the latter, kept quite clean—the old pantry or store room is one kitchen, and the milk or small entry behind, another with stoves attached. The portico and part of the gallery in the rear of the house are broken down, but the oaks and magnolias are there and notwithstanding the air of desolation around, the place is really beautiful still and could again be made into a charming residence. As soon as it was known that I had arrived the Negroes, and they are nearly all there, hastened to the front gallery to see me and shake hands as of yore—all seemed rejoiced and it would be difficult to tell you all the questions as to "Mistress" and the children and "Miss Mary." I showed them your photographs—such exclamations and why did I not bring for them those of "Master Willie" and "Toos" and Otis and Robert. I will reserve the messages they send for another time. Many of them have brot in little things they have picked and saved for you—some of which you will be glad to have. My table was supplied during the week I remained with their little presents of eggs, butter, chickens and sweet potatoes. But I will have to give you further details on another occasion, as my letter, I see, is becoming of formidable length.

Hall's next letter to his wife, which is written in French, describes the military situation at Magnolia Mound and tells of his success in getting a tenant for the plantation. We learn that cotton has now replaced sugar cane as the main crop.

New Orleans
28 February, 1865

My dear Emma,

. . . Since my last letter, I went to the house for a few days. I had trouble getting there, and I have been back for about a week. The pickets (they are called "vedettes" in french, I believe) occupy the avenue in front and on the side of the house and behind it all the way to the woods, and one is not allowed to pass through to enter or leave our home without the permission of the Commanding General. The cavalry is there night and day, good or bad weather, and the guard is changed every two hours. I was, so to speak, in prison during my stay. There are, here and in the surrounding areas, more than 15,000 soldiers—stockades on the high ground behind. As you see, our old home, once so peaceful, has become a military camp. Part of our property is within the lines and part is outside of the lines. We are protected from the "Raiders," however, which we feel is an advantage for the farming if someone wants to risk it; and I have done the impossible, as you can well imagine, and have finally succeeded in finding a tenant to take it over, but for a very small rental charge—seven thousand piastres in greenbacks, payable in advance. We will do the same thing for two years and under the same conditions. The tenant will also buy the animals that they have left me, but he will not be able to pay for them until after the cotton is harvested. Let us hope that he will be able to farm, harvest, and then pay up—the fortunes of war! This is better than nothing and I feel more relieved than I can tell you. He also pays all the taxes—levees, roads, etc.

I went down on a steamer, with eight hundred soldiers on board and three or four hundred cavalry horses. There are large troop movements at this time. Twenty-five or thirty thousand men have landed below the city lately. Thirty steamers have arrived since the first of March. We heard this morning that a steamer is arriving from Cairo [Illinois] with fifteen wagon loads of mail. It is possible that I will receive news from you tomorrow. I don't know how I will send this letter to you. I forgot to tell you that I had several paintings and four hundred books brought here, and I really do not know what to do with them. As far as furniture is concerned, it is a liability; everyone wants to sell theirs, consequently it goes for nothing and the expense of moving is enormous. The carriage was left out in the rain and sun and is not suitable for driving down the Boulevard—therefore I will not send it to you. I will try to find a buyer for it for you. I managed with great difficulty to get your piano back—it was in the hands of an officer's wife who had received it from a general and I almost got into trouble with several of these fine people, friends of the lady who supported her rights of possession. I did have it brought to the home of Mr. Bonnecaze, where I think it will be safe—since he is Consul for the King of France. The stores here are full of beautiful pianos as well as beautiful furniture for sale, and I don't know what can be done about it. Money is extremely rare, and things are much worse than last year. . . .

> Good-bye for tonight,
> GEORGE

In April of 1865 Hall wrote to his wife concerning the disposal of the furniture at Magnolia Mound. He apparently had been quite ill.

New Orleans—April 29, 1865

My dear Emma,

. . . I continue to recover rapidly from the effects of my malady, tho' still feeble and very thin. I have not yet been out of my room and as you may suppose am very tired of it. . . . The marks on my face disappear very slowly and I presume I shall be embellished by them for a couple of months to come. I had hoped to leave by the N. York Steamer of the 6th to meet the Liverpool Steamer of the 17th May, but I do not think it is possible to manage it as I have yet many things to attend to and besides it really now looks as if we were soon to have peace. . . .

I have found it impossible to sell anything at any price and will leave the remaining furniture on the plantation in charge of Mr. Nelson who rents the place and who seems a careful man. By the by, his wife was a Miss Edwards who was at the Convent at St. James when Mathilde and Sissy went there and a younger Sister recollects them both. The River is now very high and many crevasses, one of which had over-flowed nearly the whole of west Baton Rouge. I understand Mr. Nelson is at work at our levee and the side levees. How fortunate that I leased it out, but I fear that Cotton will go so low that he will not be able to pay his notes, nor the rent, as agreed, for the two coming years. Such a state of desolation as the whole country is in, you cannot imagine. It is almost universal and utter ruination to everyone and such a state of things, *in all respects*, that I cannot help repeating to you how happy, happy are they who are not here! And the future looks, if possible, still more discouraging. . . .

Love,
GEORGE

The war did soon come to an end. On May 26, a surrender by the Confederate armies west of the Mississippi was signed by General Simon Buckner, acting for General Kirby Smith. The documents were signed June 2 by General Smith, and the war was officially over. Unlike many nearby plantations, Magnolia Mound had survived the Civil War.

In 1866 Hall once more returned to Louisiana. He described his trip to his daughter Mathilde.

New Orleans, 3rd February, 1866

. . . At Cairo [Illinois] I embarked on a steamer and glided down the "Father of Waters," about 1,000 miles to New Orleans in five days. We stopped at Vicksburg and I saw on the eminences, overhanging the river, part of the line of forts and defences where our countrymen made so many thousands of the enemy found their graves. I had a good view, in passing, of our plantation, the old house on the hill looked as pretty as ever, nearly hid among the oaks and magnolias, but desolate, no smoke from the chimneys or signs of life around. I found New Orleans crowded and immense quantities of cotton arriving. Most of the old population who had survived the contest have returned but nearly all are in deep mourning. Your aunt Celeste is here—she is very thin and changed, her little boy is a fine child, he is named *Shiloh* from the battlefield on which his father was killed. . . .

After remaining here a few days I went up the river to Baton Rouge where I spent a week. I found the plantation in charge of an old german, who had been engaged to take care of it. Some thirty or forty of our old negroes are still there—they all send kind remembrances to you all. Poor creatures they are very idle and very miserable and express their regret for the good old times when they were as happy as they would desire. Many of them have died. I am endeavoring to find a tenant for the place. The sugar cane, you know, is no longer cultivated up there—only cotton. All my old friends around have either died or been killed and my visit a very melancholy one. In rambling over our grounds I stumbled on a grave-yard on the Highland Road near Cherokee Hill where hundreds of Federals were buried, mostly officers by the inscriptions on the boards. They had been killed at the battle under Breckinridge's attack of which you read the account. All the beautiful trees I had taken such care of in this direction have been cut down. . . .

God bless you.

Your affectionate father

George and Emma Hall and their children never again lived at Magnolia Mound. He sold the plantation in 1869, and he and his family continued to live in Europe. He died in Paris in 1880, and was buried at Orleans, France, where his wife Emma died in 1888. His sons returned to the United States and lived in California; his daughters remained in France, where their descendants live today.

The years following the Civil War were difficult ones. The era from the end of the war until the end of Federal occupation has been labeled with the misnomer "Reconstruction." Political confusion and upheaval, racial tension, currency problems, and economic chaos characterized this period. Although Louisiana was readmitted into the Union in 1868, Federal troops occupied the state until 1877.

Baton Rouge suffered its share of damage during the war from shelling, fire, looting, and neglect. Many of its inhabitants moved away, and some never returned. A large number of freed Negroes left the farms where they had lived as slaves and came to Baton Rouge. In 1860 the town had been almost 70 percent white; by 1880 there were 4,282 Negroes and 2,915 whites.

Most property owners in the South experienced financial setbacks as a result of the war, and George Hall was no exception. Property values had declined sharply. Magnolia Mound had been assessed in 1860 as being worth $100,000. During the time that Magnolia Mound was occupied by Federal troops, no crops were produced, the main house was looted, the sugar house and other buildings were damaged or destroyed, the sugar house machinery was destroyed, fences were torn down, and the livestock was taken. Hall sold the plantation in 1869 to Helen Walworth McCullen for $37,800. It is remarkable not only that Hall could find a buyer able to purchase the entire plantation but also that the buyer was a young woman who had lived in Baton Rouge prior to the beginning of the Civil War.

From the census and other records of the period, we are able to piece together some information about Helen Walworth McCullen. In 1860 she was fourteen years old, living in East Baton Rouge Parish. She was born in Indiana, and was the adopted daughter of Horace F. Walworth, aged 64, a native of New York. He was a farmer who at that time owned some property in Baton Rouge, including a number of lots on Highland Road. The census also tells us that he was blind. He apparently died in 1865, leaving some property to Helen. By this time she had married James McCullen, about ten years her senior, who with his family had emigrated from Ireland to Shreveport in 1850. Because the couple purchased Magnolia Mound in Helen Walworth McCullen's name, we can assume that she put up the majority of the money.

The McCullens sold the plantation in 1874 to Carl Kohn, but repurchased it in 1876 with two other investors. The other owners of the property were Charles Wieck and Mrs. Christine Redwitz. In the partnership agreement it was stated that Charles Wieck would keep books of accounts on all plantation business and that Mrs. Redwitz would make advances of money and supplies for cultivation. James McCullen's duties were to manage Magnolia Mound and see to its cultivation, which he did until his

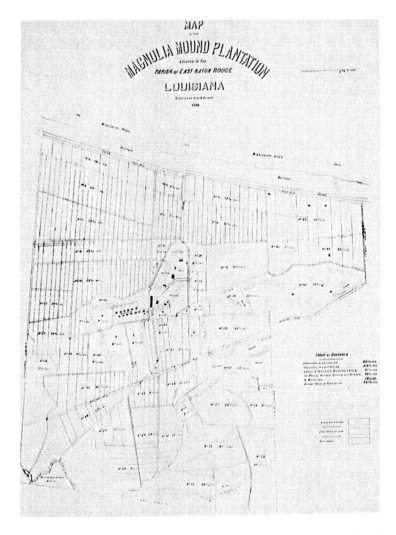

Figure 10. The 1880 map of the grounds of Magnolia Mound showed the various land uses on the plantation. The main house is the black square closest to the river in the center of the map.

death in 1880. During this time the sugar house machinery was repaired, and the property once again became an efficient working plantation, producing both cotton and sugarcane. The 1880 map (figure 10) shows the location of the residence, the sugar house, and the quarter houses.

Franklin Brooks, Jr., was the manager of Magnolia Mound under McCullen's supervision during the 1870s, a position which he held until 1883. He and his family occupied the plantation house during this period. His granddaughter, Inez Dearing Searles, remembers events that took place when her mother, Inez Brooks, lived there. (Inez Brooks married Emmett C. Dearing in a ceremony at Magnolia Mound.) Many of her recollections reflect the lifestyle of earlier days on the plantation. She went to school at St. Joseph's Academy, where she and her two sisters would board during the week, coming home on the weekends and holidays. Her family spoke both French and English. Her father spent much of his time in the fields on horseback. They, as all other occupants of river plantations, were concerned when the waters of the Mississippi began to rise. On one occasion the high waters threatened to break through the levee, and all who were at the plantation worked day and night on the levee until the waters receded.

Thus we see the end of the Civil War and Reconstruction years and the beginning of an era of greater prosperity. Magnolia Mound continued to be an attractive financial investment; however, the plantation property soon evolved from a working plantation to a real estate investment.

CHAPTER VII

❀◉❀

The Developers

In the late nineteenth century, Baton Rouge began to emerge from the ashes of the Civil War and Reconstruction. It was a time of political conservatism and economic development. The state capital was moved back to Baton Rouge in 1882. Roads were improved, railroads were built, levees were repaired, and new levees were constructed by a newly appointed board of state engineers. Interest in public education began to grow, and an institution of higher learning, Louisiana State University and A. & M. College, was housed in the Pentagon Barracks.

Magnolia Mound, as an established working plantation, was an excellent investment opportunity. After James McCullen's death, Magnolia Mound was bought in 1883 by Carl Redwitz, who owned the plantation for two years before selling it to August Strenzke, Edward Witting, Henry Shorten, and Louis Barillier. Barillier, who bought out his partners in 1889, would with his family be the last owner of Magnolia Mound to operate it as a cotton and sugar plantation.

Louis Barillier was born in Switzerland in 1830. His parents emigrated to the United States when he was an infant. He was originally a butcher, but through wise investment of his money he eventually became a planter.

Figure 11. The Hart House, situated behind Magnolia Mound plantation home, now houses offices of the Magnolia Mound staff. *(Photograph by Jim Mitchell)*

He married Elezene Kinner in 1853; they were the parents of twelve children. His son Louis and his wife Bena Cunningham Barillier, who lived at Magnolia Mound, had three daughters. One, Ella, married John B. Aucoin, who became overseer of the plantation. The Aucoins had two children, who were also born at Magnolia Mound. At the time of the senior Louis Barillier's death in 1903, his estate, which included large tracts of valuable property in several Baton Rouge locations, was appraised at almost $100,000; Magnolia Mound alone was valued at $25,000.

Barillier's heirs sold Magnolia Mound to Robert A. Hart in 1904 for $42,000. From a prominent Baton Rouge family, Hart was an extremely successful businessman, and was active in public affairs for years. He was on the school board, serving as its president, and was the financial head of the police jury. He was also mayor from 1898 to 1902, a term marked by real progress for the town of Baton Rouge. Under his direction, bonds were passed to provide money to improve and pave streets, improve drainage, and build schools.

Robert Hart was a bachelor, and he built a home for himself several hundred yards behind the old plantation home. Known as the Hart house, his home is now owned by the Baton Rouge Parks and Recreation Commission (figure 11). Hart made the original plantation home available to his relatives, and several of them lived in the house over the years. Mrs. Gertrude Hart Aldrich, Hart's niece, and her sons lived there after her husband's death. Later, Mrs. Belle Hart Bynum and her son occupied the house.

Magnolia Mound was a working plantation when Hart bought it. Baton Rouge followed the national trend toward urbanization, however, and as the town grew southward, the real estate value of the property escalated. By 1929 Hart had subdivided most of the 800 acres, retaining only the two houses and 75 acres (figure 12).

Figure 12. A 1928 rear view of the main house shows its deteriorated condition.

The twenty-five years that Hart owned Magnolia Mound were eventful ones. Standard Oil built a refinery in Baton Rouge in 1909, beginning an industry that continues to be vital to the city and to the nation. In the 1920s Louisiana State University began building its present campus on property known as the Gartness plantation, located next door to Magnolia Mound. In 1928 a progressive age in politics evolved as Huey Long started his controversial career as governor of Louisiana. In 1929 the depression hit Baton Rouge, as it did the rest of the nation.

Hart sold his two houses and seventy-five acres that were left of Magnolia Mound to his niece, Miss Marie Blanche Duncan, in 1929. Miss Duncan developed part of the property as the Magnolia Terrace subdivision, but kept eight acres, the Hart House, and the original plantation house.

Baton Rouge slowly recovered from the depression and experienced an economic upturn as the nation geared up for World War II in 1941. In the late 1940s Miss Duncan and her cousin, Mrs. Claude Reynaud, operated a gift and antique shop in the plantation house for about a year. At that time the house was still not equipped with electricity or running water.

In 1951, Miss Duncan contracted with the architectural firm of Goodman and Miller to renovate the old plantation home. A subfloor was added, electricity installed, bathrooms put in, and extensive repairs made. After the renovations were completed, Dr. Robert P. Ball and his family lived there, in 1951 and 1952.

Miss Duncan died in 1958 and left the property to her cousin, Mrs. John Anderson, the former Anna Belle Hart, who took her residence at the Hart House. The last Hart family members to live at Magnolia Mound were Mrs. Belle Hart Bynum and her son, Hart. After their deaths in the early 1960s the house was unoccupied. The plantation home inevitably began to assume an air of disrepair and neglect.

Mrs. Anderson offered the house for sale and after some time found a buyer, Al German, a real estate developer. The old plantation house that had been home to so many families, that had survived the Civil War and Reconstruction, when so many other houses were destroyed, was to be demolished so that an apartment complex could be constructed on its site.

PART III

CHAPTER VIII

⊰◉⊱

The Rescue

The recent history of the preservation movement is truly phenomenal. Rooted in earlier philanthropic restorations, such as Colonial Williamsburg, the interest in the past and preserving it is a dominant force in our society today. An enormous investment of energy, intellect, and money, on both the private and public level, is being expended in this direction.

With a few exceptions, Baton Rouge's record in preserving its colonial past can only be described as dismal. Much has been lost, not solely in Baton Rouge but elsewhere as well, in the name of "progress." Historically and architecturally significant structures have disappeared to make way for offices and apartment buildings, expressways, and the ubiquitous parking lot.

Magnolia Mound almost suffered the fate of the wrecking ball and bulldozer. The story of its rescue contains elements of true drama and images of actively involved citizens defiantly working to halt the dismantling of the structure. Workmen had begun to pry loose the finely carved Adam-style mantelpiece in the parlor (figure 13) and were stacking the classically detailed dentil and reed-and-ribbon molding on the front gallery when neighbors hurriedly summoned help. Two attorneys made an

Figure 13. The Baton Rouge *Morning Advocate* featured this photograph of workmen tearing out the mantel in 1965 before
Magnolia Mound rescue attempts succeeded. *(Staff photograph by John Boss)*

after-hours visit to a district judge, and a temporary
restraining order was obtained to halt demolition long
enough for preservation groups to explore possibilities of
saving the landmark house.

At this time the house had been vacant for several years,
presenting an unkempt appearance when viewed from
Nicholson Drive, with tangled underbrush obscuring all
but a fleeting and shadowy glimpse of the house itself.

Through the years, local legend entwined the name of
Prince Murat, nephew of Napoleon and colorful bon
vivant, with that of the old house. Gradually it was his
name that became attached to it, rather than the historically accurate name that appeared in legal records as
far back as 1804.

By early 1965, the fledgling Foundation for Historical Louisiana, only two years old, focused on Magnolia Mound in its program of landmark preservation. But before the foundation could act, a Texas land developer acquired an option to buy the house and the remaining eight acres and applied for rezoning to allow the construction of multistory apartments. The protest was immediate from leaders of civic, cultural, and professional organizations throughout the state. The Foundation for Historical Louisiana reacted quickly in marshaling support. Public pressure mounted, and the whole *cause célèbre* had city councilmen treading gingerly on the issue.

Then began one of the bitterest zoning conflicts the city had witnessed in years. The battle lines were drawn and the troops were mustered in a scenario that has been enacted countless times in countless locales—business acumen versus cultural heritage.

Cultural heritage won this round. On the night that the zoning issue came before the council, the city courtroom was packed with preservation groups primed to testify. The surprise announcement that the application for rezoning had been withdrawn was almost an anticlimax. Evidently the strong opposition had been effective, and the announcement was a bow to the inevitable.

But a happy ending was not yet in sight. Although the land could not be used for apartments, the property was purchased on the day the option expired. A period of intense activity was then initiated by the preservationists to work out a feasible plan to save the late eighteenth-century structure. Negotiations between the developer and a citizens' group failed. Mayor W. W. Dumas, a strong supporter, appointed a twenty-six-member committee to study the problem. Contacts were made with the Louisiana legislative delegation, the governor, the national congressional delegation, the National Trust for Historic Preservation, and other influential forces.

The mayor learned that a Housing and Urban Development open space grant was available, raising the hope that the problem of financing the purchase of the property could be solved. The Recreation and Park Commission for the Parish of East Baton Rouge (BREC), the logical city-parish agency to take title to the property, authorized an appraisal as a basis for a cash offer made to the new owner.

Into this charged atmosphere came the notice that the dismantling of the house had begun. When BREC's initial offer was rejected, expropriation proceedings were begun as the only remaining alternative. At issue in the case was the assessment of the value of the property, in view of its historical significance. In the four days of testimony presented by Ashton Stewart, the attorney for BREC, much of the connection of Prince Murat with Magnolia Mound was steadily refuted. However, on December 24, 1966, BREC acquired Magnolia Mound for $209,680, and after appeal the price was reduced to $169,680, the appraisal value offered by BREC before the suit.

The rescue was now a *fait accompli.* The saving of this historic house and grounds was an excellent example of how an aroused citizens' group could solicit the cooperation of local, state, and federal agencies and achieve rather quickly a specific result.

CHAPTER IX

⚜️

The Restoration

If the rescue had its dramatic moments, the restoration was a contrasting story of hard, often unheralded, work by many dedicated people. BREC retained ownership of the land, and the Foundation for Historical Louisiana assumed the financial responsibility of restoring and furnishing the house and administering its operation when it was opened to the public.

In 1972 Magnolia Mound was officially designated on the National Register of Historic Places. Restoration was begun under the supervision of a board of trustees appointed by the Foundation. George Leake, a restoration architect from New Orleans, was engaged to design and supervise the restoration, which took three long years to complete.

Although the sturdy cypress structural members of the house were still in remarkable condition, the toll of time and neglect left much to be done (figure 14). Through the years interior changes had been made, including the extensive renovations done in the 1950s that made the house more livable in accordance with modern tastes. The intent and purpose from the beginning was to recreate Magnolia Mound as a historic house museum, to serve the educational function of presenting a picture of the past.

Figure 14. Magnolia Mound during the early stages of restoration. The roof was repaired first to slow the devastating effects of rain and bad weather. (*Photograph by Vaughn Glasgow*)

The first step in proper restoration is research, and a good restoration, if based on historical accuracy, is a formidable task. It is necessary to find out who lived in a house, when they lived there, and through the lives of the occupants trace the social history of the structure. A Magnolia Mound research team consequently began the arduous work of digging through conveyance records, deeds, succession records, and land plats. The decision followed to turn the house back to its appearance and function of the time span from 1800 to 1830, roughly the period of the residency of the Armand Duplantiers.

The restorer of a historic house can call himself blessed if the original records compiled during construction of the house still exist. Many of the later plantation houses, such as Rosedown and Nottaway, had builders who left careful records. If mantels, hardware, or chandeliers were missing, the records occasionally gave clues to their original appearance.

Lacking written records, as in the case of Magnolia Mound, many different disciplines can be used to unlock the mysteries of the house. Much can be learned from the structure itself. For the architectural historian, construction techniques can tell a story and help date when construction took place. The mortise-and-tenon and pegged construction techniques of Magnolia Mound were proof of its early vintage, and the mud-and-moss or *bousillage* infill marked it with probability as late eighteenth century. The research in legal records pinpointed the construction of the original four-room settler's house as between 1791 and 1798. Examination proved that additions to the house were made in the early nineteenth century rather than the late nineteenth century, the assumption early in the restoration. This meant that it had been Armand and Constance Duplantier who enlarged the space to include the dining room, plantation office, and two bedrooms, to accommodate the six children from their former marriages and the five more children to come. In order to take their place in the social milieu of Baton Rouge in the early 1800s, embellishments such as the handsome coved ceiling, finely carved mantel, and moldings were added to the parlor, creating a proper setting for formal entertaining.

Unexpected discoveries can result in triumphant moments in restoration work. As records were lacking to give guidance on color schemes and other decorating touches for Magnolia Mound, the discovery of a scrap of faded wallpaper underneath the parlor molding was quite an exciting find. It was a definite bit of serendipity when experts in the field of decorative arts identified this wallpaper as having been made around 1810 in France. It was therefore imperative that this wallpaper be reproduced in order to be included in the parlor. Ordering this special paper from France and installing it probably had been the crowning touch in the Duplantiers' redecorating project. The original color of the cove ceiling and the woodwork was determined by paint scrapings and was produced as closely as possible in modern paint (figure 15).

If top quality research is a goal, archaeological investigations can add to the accumulation of knowledge. An early dig at Magnolia Mound, which examined the foundation structure and the area under the house, located some of the former pathways. A later investigation located the probable site of the kitchen. Through archaeology one can also learn about life in a house—every generation leaves traces of itself in the dirt, and the artifacts turned up can chronicle the social and cultural history of the house. From the Magnolia Mound kitchen dig came prehistoric pottery, a Spanish coin, shards of mochaware pottery, china and wine bottles from the early 1800s, and Minié balls from the Civil War period.

Bit by bit the clues were gathered, the knowledge analyzed, and the work slowly completed. In 1975 the

Figure 15. The restored parlor in Magnolia Mound features documented wallpaper and paint colors; note also the cove ceiling. *(Photograph by Frank Lotz Miller)*

restored Magnolia Mound house, sparsely furnished, was opened to the public on a limited basis.

The restorer of a historic house can call himself doubly blessed if he is lucky enough to acquire furniture owned by the family in the selected time period. Again, many plantation owners left detailed inventories of purchases of furniture, silver, draperies, and paintings. Lacking either original furniture or inventories for Magnolia Mound, research was again the answer. As an example, a document in the Pointe Coupee courthouse dated February 12, 1793, yielded some choice clues. This record of the probate sale of the estate of Claude

Trenonay revealed that Armand Duplantier, his nephew, purchased a large and varied selection of items, some of which could have been included in the furnishings at Magnolia Mound after Duplantier's marriage to Constance Rochon Joyce. His sophisticated taste is reflected in his selection of crystal compotes, twelve dozen faience plates, two faience soup tureens, forty-six small glasses for liqueur, and four ceramic chandeliers. His practicality is reflected in the purchase of tools, livestock, and slaves, as well as nine pairs of nankeen pants and four pairs of drawers ("some good and some not good"), and one black hat.

Newspaper advertisements describing merchant's wares, inventories from other houses of the same era, and travelers' accounts describing houses visited also contribute to a picture of what could have been in the rooms at Magnolia Mound. Slowly, furnishings have been selected until now the collection incorporates one of the most comprehensive public collections of pre-1830 Louisiana-made furniture.

Another bit of serendipity involving detective work was the discovery of the late nineteenth-century overseer's house. This began with the discovery of an 1880 survey map of the plantation that indicated all structures, roads, drainage canals, and even a cemetery. This was blown up as a transparent overlay for an enlargement of a present-day map of Baton Rouge. The main house fell right into place, as did Blundon Home Orphanage, which was built on the foundation of the old sugar house. The search was then on in the neighborhoods now around Magnolia Mound for any other structure originally belonging to the plantation that might have survived. One old house on Vermont Street was particularly interesting, because the portico or gallery faced toward Magnolia Mound rather than the present-day street, and its construction definitely appeared much older than nearby houses. Using the 1880 map, this house fell exactly where the structure assumed to be the overseer's house should have been located. After several years, the house was acquired and moved onto the present property.

The reproduction of a working kitchen of the early 1800s was completed in 1979 (figure 16). This addition, funded by the Junior League of Baton Rouge and the city-parish goverment, augments the educational goals in depicting the culture and lifestyle of this period. Research in legal records, visits to kitchens of the same period, and the use of old materials all contributed to its authentic appearance. Weekly cooking demonstrations, using old recipes, authentic cookware, and methods, add color and life to the interpretive program (figure 17).

It is a remarkable fact that eight hundred acres of the original plantation remained intact until after 1904. However, its dissolution was rapid as urbanization reached out after that time. Curiously, that process is now reversed, and the old plantation lands are now experiencing a small renaissance. With the acquisition of the

Figure 16. The reproduction working kitchen is situated to the rear of the main house.

Figure 17. Weekly cooking demonstrations in the kitchen feature old
cookware, recipes, and methods. *(Photograph by Frank
Lotz Miller)*

adjacent Hart property in 1979, the eight acres that
surrounded Magnolia Mound when restoration began
have now grown to over thirteen acres of the original land
grant. With the old grove of live oaks that still shelter the
house and the establishment of a kitchen garden and crop
garden, some of the feeling of plantation scenes can be
evoked.

"Here is a rare survivor which is part and parcel of the
fabric of the Louisiana story," wrote one advocate for the
restoration in a letter to a local newspaper during the
zoning controversy. That is the most apt description of all
for Magnolia Mound—a survivor. Once again the laughter
of children echoes over the grounds as school groups tour.
As in the early 1800s, visitors traveling on the river by

Figure 18. This Magnolia Mound room is furnished as the primary
bedchamber. *(Photograph by Frank Lotz Miller)*

steamboat come to pay a visit. Docents from the Mound
Builders, a volunteer organization, receive visitors,
dressed in authentic period day dresses, and provide a
guided and narrated tour (figure 18). On special occasions, when the Mound is decorated once again for an
evening party, the gallery doors are opened wide to
receive guests, soft candlelight illuminating the interior.
The old house lives on.

Bibliography

Unpublished Material

Allen, Frederick Stuart. "A Social and Economic History of Baton Rouge: 1850–1860." Master's thesis, Louisiana State University, 1936.

Baton Rouge. Clerk of Court's Office. *Archives of the Spanish Government of West Florida.* vols. 1–4, 11 (translated by the Works Progress Administration, 1937–38). This collection provides information on Hillin, Joyce, and Duplantier. Copies of these documents are also found in the Magnolia Mound research files and in the Stewart Papers, Louisiana State University Library Archives.

Baton Rouge. East Baton Rouge Parish Courthouse. "Certification of the Marriage Record of Constance Rochon Joyce and Armand Duplantier," included in translated Spanish West Florida records, vol. 3, p. 374. The courthouse also possesses the conveyance records for Magnolia Mound and the Gartness plantation.

Baton Rouge. East Baton Rouge Parish Library, Louisiana State Library, and Louisiana State University Library. U.S. Census records for East Baton Rouge Parish, 1850 to 1880 and 1900; for Caddo Parish, 1850.

Baton Rouge. Louisiana State University Library Archives. Stewart Papers, These unpublished papers, collected by Ashton Stewart, are copies of early documents regarding the ownership of Magnolia Mound, conveyance records of Magnolia Mound and Gartness plantation up to the 1960s, and the sources used to determine the price of Magnolia Mound when it was expropriated.

Baton Rouge. Magnolia Mound plantation research files. The collection of material deposited in the files at the plantation embraces a wide field of topics connected in some way to the history of the plantation. In addition to copies of documents and records deposited in other collections, there are a number of items of interest to the plantation historian.

Bannon, Lois. Interview with Inez Dearing (Mrs. Richard J.) Searles, 1976. Mrs. Searles's grandfather, Franklin Brooks, Jr., was the manager of Magnolia Mound plantation in the late nineteenth century.

Barrow, Augustine Reynaud. "Constance and Armand Duplantier." Mrs. Barrow, a great, great granddaughter of Armand Duplantier, wrote this twentieth-century unpublished paper for the Daughters of the American Revolution.

Burden, Eileen K., and Gagliano, Sherwood M. "Archaeological Excavation at Magnolia Mound: A Search for the 1830 Kitchen." 1977.

Byrd, Winifred. Interview with Fannie Bailey (Mrs. Claude) Reynaud. Mrs. Reynaud, a relative of Robert Hart, related information on the last families that lived at Magnolia Mound.

Cash, Cynthia. "Study for Master Site Development Plan for Magnolia Mound Plantation." 1981. This paper includes information on daily life in antebellum Louisiana; it was used extensively in Chapter 5.

Castille, George J. "Archaeological Testing of Portions of Magnolia Mound Plantation." 1981.

Emerson, Jon. "Master Site Development Plan for Magnolia Mound Plantation." 1981 (Unicorn Studio).

Greene, Charles M. "Map of the Magnolia Mound Plantation, located in the Parish of East Baton Rouge, Louisiana, 1880." A copy of this map, made from the original owned by Mrs. Annabelle Hart Anderson, is in the possession of Magnolia Mound.

Haag, William G. "Some Archaeological Investigations at Magnolia Mound House." 1973–74. The earliest modern dig at Magnolia Mound concentrated on foundations and the area under the house.

Hall Family Letters, 1857–66. These letters, covering the period when the Halls owned Magnolia Mound, are quoted extensively in chapters 5 and 6.

Thom, Evelyn Martindale, compiler. "Magnolia Mound—Murat House." 1965–68. A collection of newspaper clippings and photographs on the rescue of Magnolia Mound, gathered for the Baton Rouge Foundation for Historical Louisiana, this material is used extensively for chapters 8 and 9.

Douglas, Meriel LeBrane, "Some Aspects of the Social History of Baton Rouge from 1830 to 1850." Master's thesis, Louisiana State University, 1936. This thesis provides information on Baton Rouge and its history, social life, and customs.

Mobile, Alabama. Church of Our Lady of Conception. "Book of the Baptism of Whites," folio 35 (April, 1790). The baptismal certificate of Josephine Joyce shows that she was born on March 18, 1790.

Mobile, Alabama. Probate Court. *Spanish Colonial Records,* vol. 2, pp. 14–15. This record entry concerns some Mobile property of Constance Joyce.

New Orleans. Historic New Orleans Collection. Duplantier Letters. This file contains copies of material in the private collection of the de Combarieu family of France.

New Roads, Louisiana. Pointe Coupee Parish Courthouse. *Conveyance Book 1793,* entry 1775. This document includes a list of items purchased by Armand Duplantier at the probate sale of his uncle Claude Trenonay's estate in Pointe Coupee; Trenonay's complete inventory is also listed. (The original documents are written in French, but translations are deposited in the Magnolia Mound research files.)

Rehder, John Burkhardt. "Sugar Plantation Settlements of Southern Louisiana: A Cultural Geography." Master's thesis, Louisiana State University, 1971. This paper gives architectural and agricultural information concerning early sugar plantations.

Published Material

Albrecht, Andrew C. "The Origin and Early Settlement of Baton Rouge, Louisiana." *Louisiana Historical Quarterly* 28 (January, 1945): 5–68. Useful information about the prehistoric Indians, European explorers, and the first French concession at Baton Rouge, to Diron Dartaguette, is covered in this narrative.

Andrews, J., and Higgins, W. *Creole Mobile 1702–1813.* Mobile: Bienville Historical Society, 1974. This book lists some residents of Mobile during the period from 1702 to 1813 and briefly relates biographical details.

Baton Rouge *Gazette,* October 1, 1827. Armand Duplantier's obituary is found in this issue.

Baton Rouge *State Times:* May 25 and 26, 1939. These two days cover Robert Hart's death. December 15, 1942. Stanley C. Arthur's article "Landowners on the Mississippi River during the Time of the Spanish Domination" includes an unscaled 1799 map that erroneously shows Magnolia Mound as belonging to James Hillin. John Joyce acquired it in 1798. November 15, 1956. An article on this date discusses Baton Rouge mayors.

Baton Rouge *State-Times* and Baton Rouge *Morning Advocate,* June 11 to September 25, 1965; April 2 to December 28, 1966;and June 28 to 30 and November 24 to December 24, 1967. These issues give newspaper coverage of events concerning the rezoning controversy, the expropriation suit, and the acquisition of Magnolia Mound by the Recreation and Park Commission for the Parish of East Baton Rouge (BREC).

Biographical and Historical Memoirs of Louisiana. 2 vols. Chicago: Goodspeed Publishing Co., 1892. This work gives a history of the state, a sketch of each parish, and biographical information on many noteworthy Louisiana individuals and families.

Carleton, Mark T. *River Capital: An Illustrated History of Baton Rouge.* Woodland Hills, Ca.: Windsor Publications, 1981.

Carter, Hodding, Jr. *John Law Wasn't So Wrong.* Baton Rouge: Esso Standard Oil Co., 1952. A history of Louisiana's resources, this book contains an appendix and a chronology of Louisiana history.

Colomb, R. W. "Lafayette's Visit to Baton Rouge, April, 1825." *Louisiana Historical Quarterly* 14 (April, 1931): 178–81. Translated from the French *Lafayette in America* by A. Levasseur, Lafayette's secretary, who accompanied him on his American travels.

Craven, Avery O. *Rachel of Old Louisiana.* Baton Rouge: Louisiana State University Press, 1975. This is an interesting account of the life and problems of Rachel O'Connor, a plantation owner in the St. Francisville, Louisiana, area in the 1820s. (The letters on which this volume are based are housed in the Louisiana State University Library Archives.)

Daniel, Lucia Elizabeth. "The Louisiana People's Party." *Louisiana Historical Quarterly* 26 (October, 1943): 1055–62. The condition of Louisiana following the Civil War is described in this piece.

Davis, Edwin Adams. *Heroic Years: Louisiana in the War for Southern Independence*. Baton Rouge: Bureau of Educational Materials and Research, College of Education, Louisiana State University, 1964.

_____ . *Louisiana: A Narrative History*. Baton Rouge: Claitor's Publishing Division, 1971.

_____ . *Louisiana: The Pelican State*. Baton Rouge: Louisiana State University Press, 1961.

Dawson, Sarah Morgan. *A Confederate Girl's Diary*. Westport, Conn.: Greenwood Press, 1960. Dawson provides an eyewitness account of the occupation of Baton Rouge during the Civil War (quoted in Chapter 6).

Dufour, Charles L. *Ten Flags in the Wind*. New York: Harper and Row, 1967.

East, Charles. *Baton Rouge: A Civil War Album*. Baton Rouge: Charles East, 1977. This collection of rare photographs taken in Baton Rouge during the Civil War is accompanied by text.

Favrot, J. St. Clair. *Tales of Our Town*. Baton Rouge: Louisiana National Bank, 1973. These "tales" relate the early history of Baton Rouge (directly quoted in Chapter 2).

Gayarré, Charles. "A Louisiana Plantation of the Old Regime." *Harper's New Monthly Magazine* 74 (March, 1887): 606–21. An excellent and detailed chronicler of life on an early Louisiana sugar plantation and events of the period, Gayarré also serves as a source for the account of the first successful granulation of sugar in Chapter 3.

Hamilton, Peter J. *Colonial Mobile*. Tuscaloosa: University of Alabama Press, 1976. This book contains information about land grants, contracts, and litigation during the Spanish colonial period. The coverage includes James Joyce's business affairs in the Mobile area and Constance Rochon Joyce's family.

Hanna, Alfred Jackson. "Achille Murat." *Encyclopedia Americana*, vol. 19, New York 1977, p. 602.

_____ . *A Prince in Their Midst: The Adventurous Life of Achille Murat on the American Frontier*. Norman: University of Oklahoma Press, 1946. Pages 210–211 refer to Murat's sojourn in Baton Rouge; a short quote from this source is in Chapter 4.

Holmes, Sarah Katherine. *Brokenburn: The Journal of Kate Stone, 1861–1868*. Baton Rouge: Louisiana State University Press,

1955. Quotes taken from this book on the life and problems of an overseer are used in Chapter 5.

Leach, Marguerite T. "The Aftermath of Reconstruction in Louisiana." *Louisiana Historical Quarterly* 32 (July, 1949): 631–717.

Le Page du Pratz, A. S. *The History of Louisiana.* London: T. Becket, 1774. The indigo material in Chapter 2 is from this source.

McDaniel, Hilda Mulvey. "Francis Tillou Nicholls and the End of Reconstruction." *Louisiana Historical Quarterly* 32 (April, 1949): 357–513.

McGinty, Garnie William. *A History of Louisiana.* New York: Exposition Press, 1949.

_____. "Twentieth Century Louisiana." *Louisiana Historical Quarterly* 32 (January, 1949): 5–16. This article describes life in the early 1900s.

Magruder, H. F. "Looking Backward." *Proceedings of the Historical Society of East and West Baton Rouge* 2 (1917–18): 17. A direct quote from this source concerning Achille Murat is included in Chapter 4.

Menn, Joseph Karl. *The Large Slaveholders of Louisiana—1860.* Gretna, La.: Pelican Publishing Co., 1964. Information is given on large slaveholders—those owning fifty or more slaves—in Louisiana; George Hall is mentioned in pages 139–40. Biographical and agricultural statistics are noted in tables.

Moody, V. Alton. "Slavery on Louisiana Sugar Plantations." *Louisiana Historical Quarterly* 7 (April, 1924): 191–294. Moody analyzes the sugar industry and slave labor, and details the necessities of life—housing, food, clothing, and health care—and the social and religious customs of the slaves. Some of this material is used in Chapter 5.

Morrison, Veneta de Greffenried. *Index: Early Marriages of Pointe Coupee,* 1771–1843. [s.l.: s.n. 1971.] This reference work includes information on the LeDoux family,

Myers, Rose. *A History of Baton Rouge, 1699–1812.* Baton Rouge: Louisiana State University Press, 1976. This scholarly account of the Baton Rouge area encompasses the era before and during the Hillin, Joyce, and Duplantier years.

New Orleans *Figaro,* May 26, 1976. Roulac Toledano's article, "A New Historic Neighborhood," relates that Duplantier, as an agent for

Lafayette, acquired lands to be given to the general by the United States.

New Orleans *Weekly Delta*, May 8, 1952. This paper includes a reprint of a mid-nineteenth-century letter to the editor of the Baton Rouge *Comet* that describes the archaeological dig at Magnolia Mound during Hall's ownership.

Pitot, James. *Observations on the Colony of Louisiana, from 1766 to 1802, Translated from the French with an Introduction by Henry C. Pitot.* Baton Rouge: Louisiana State University Press, for the Historic New Orleans Collection, 1979. Direct quotations about tobacco and cotton production in Chapter 2 are from this book.

Pointe Coupee Banner, October 30, 1980; August 13 and 20, 1981. Articles cover the history of the LeDoux family and their descendants, written by Michael Dagries Wynne.

Robin, C. C. *Voyage to Louisiana, 1803–5.* Gretna, La.: Pelican Publishing Co., 1966. This abridged translation by Stuart O. Landry, Jr., covers commerce, industry, and trade in Louisiana. Far from being a dry account of economics, however, and despite the author's nationalistic bias, the work presents a wealth of detail on customs and lifestyle. This book is a source for material on clothing and fashions, imports, and goods cited in Chapter 3.

Scarborough, William Kauffman. *The Overseer: Plantation Management in the Old South.* Baton Rouge: Louisiana State University Press, 1966. This book discusses the overseer's role on the plantation, and his duties and responsibilities.

Seale, William. *Recreating the Historic House Interior.* Nashville: American Association for State and Local History, 1979. This text examines research techniques that apply to all aspects of historic house restoration. It is an excellent source book for recreating interiors with accuracy by basing the work on professional historical research.

Seip, Terry. "Municipal Politics and the Negro: Baton Rouge 1865–1888." In *Readings in Louisiana Politics,* edited by Mark T. Carleton, Perry H. Howard, and Joseph B. Parker, pp. 242–66. Baton Rouge: Claitor's Publishing Division, 1975. This narrative provides information on Reconstruction government and politics in Baton Rouge.

Sibley, John. "The Journal of Dr. John Sibley, July-October, 1802." *Louisiana Historical Quarterly* 10 (October, 1927): 474–97. This day-by-day chronicle of an upriver journey affords graphic material on people, furnishings, plantation life, and topography of the period (used in Chapter 3).

_____ . Letters of Dr. John Sibley to His Son Samuel Hopkins Sibley, 1803–1821." *Louisiana Historical Quarterly* 10 (October, 1927): 498–507. A letter dated February, 1803, describes an overnight visit to a Louisiana river plantation home (an extensive quote is used in Chapter 3).

Stirling, David Lee, ed. "New Orleans, 1801: An Account by John Pintard." *Louisiana Historical Quarterly* 34 (July, 1951): 217–33. This source is used extensively for material in Chapter 3 on life-style and customs. The original manuscript is deposited with the New York Historical Society and was the basis for a series of six articles published in the New York *Daily Advertiser,* May 15 to 22, 1802.

Thom, Evelyn Martindale. *Baton Rouge Story: An Historical Sketch of Louisiana's Capital City.* Baton Rouge: Baton Rouge Foundation for Historical Louisiana, 1967.

Thomas, LaVerne III. *LeDoux: A Pioneer Franco-American Family with Detailed Sketches of Allied Families.* New Orleans: Polyanthos, 1982. Information is given on the lives of Emma LeDoux Hall and George Hall and their descendants. Excerpts from letters written by members of the family are included.

Wilson, Samuel, and Lehman, Bernard. *New Orleans Architecture: The Lower Garden District.* Gretna, La.: Pelican Publishing Co., 1971. Pages 2, 9, 13, and 15 concern Duplantier's ownership of the Delord-Sarpy plantation.

Index

Printed in the United States
1475600001B/376-396